XB

Nichi Hodgson is a journalist, broadcaster, and author living in London. She regularly contributes to the *Guardian*, *Vice*, and the *Telegraph* on civil liberties and censorship issues, sex and the law, and gender politics. She writes for US women's mag Bustle.com on US politics, social policy, and health, and was for some time the *Men's Health* Sexual Adventurer columnist. Nichi was one of the first British journalists to court-report via Twitter, and is cited in Wikipedia for her coverage of the 2012 obscenity trial, R v Peacock. Nichi is a regular commentator on BBC Radio 2's *The Jeremy Vine Show*, BBC Radio 5 Live and BBC Radio 4's *Woman's Hour*, and she has made a documentary on the ethics of porn for BBC Radio 4. She reviews the papers and comments regularly for *Sky News*, and makes frequent appearances in TV documentaries and debates on sex, porn and society. Her first book, *Bound to You*, a BDSM memoir, is published by Hodder.

The Curious History of Dating

Nichi Hodgson

ROBINSON

ROBINSON

First published in Great Britain in 2017 by Robinson

1 3 5 7 9 10 8 6 4 2

A CIP catalogue record for this book
is available from the British Library.

ISBN: 978-1-47213-806-4

Typeset in Century by Hewer Text UK Ltd, Edinburgh
Printed and bound in Great Britain by Clays Ltd, St Ives plc

Papers used by Robinson are from well-managed
forests and other responsible sources.

MIX
Paper from
responsible sources
FSC
www.fsc.org FSC® C104740

Robinson
An imprint of
Little, Brown Book Group
Carmelite House
50 Victoria Embankment
London EC4Y 0DZ

An Hachette UK Company
www.hachette.co.uk

www.littlebrown.co.uk

For Richard

Contents

Chapter One

The 1700s : The estate of your heart

In 1786, it was a truth universally acknowledged that a single man in possession of a large fortune could find a wife via a Lonely Hearts ad, published in *The Times* newspaper. In fact, Lonely Hearts ads had actually existed for around a hundred years by the time any of Mr Darcy's contemporaries jumped on the hay cart. When the Licensing Act of 1662, which regulated the press, ended, posting for a wife, or for a husband for a daughter, slowly started to take off and, by the end of the eighteenth century, this sort of thing was appearing in *The Times* on a daily basis: 'A Gentleman of very considerable fortune, about the age of forty, offers himself as an Husband to any well-educated, amiable and agreeable Lady of good character and not more than 30 years of age, and as much younger as may be, who will undertake to exercise those attentions which his particular situation requires.'

It might sound like speed-dating, Georgian-style, but posting a Lonely Hearts ad was about as far removed from easy access as today's dating apps are from decorum. Dating via personal ads consisted of a lot of letter-writing, sighing, hoping, and waiting for a reply to one's mailbox, which was often a coffee house or inn where single ladies of an upstanding reputation were not to stray. This meant enlisting the help of a trusted male envoy who could deliver

1

and collect replies on your behalf, at least until the 1780s when shops, newspaper offices and libraries became the main holding houses. Answering personal ads was a furtive business and good girls were not to be seen going at it.

The age of consent may only have been twelve at the time that Jane Austen was writing (first set out in English law in 1275), but female chastity, modesty and dignity were not only expected but required in order for a lady to make a good match. Prior to the Regency period, most relationship advice published in courtesy books was written by men, for men. But as women became the predominant writers and readers of their age, so did they take ownership of the courtship script. In a so-called model reply from mother to daughter on the subject of dating, published in *The Complete Letter-writer* in 1800, the mother advises: 'Nine or ten years is what one might call the natural term of life for beauty in a young woman. But by accidents or misbehaviour it may die long before its time . . . but keep your reputation, as you have hitherto kept it, and that will be a beauty which shall last to the end of your days.'

Physical beauty, in the form of sloping shoulders, small, high breasts, plumpness, a 'fair countenance', and minimal freckles was the Regency ideal. But just as important to 'comeliness' were virtues of character. Conversation, reading and learning for moral improvement rather than knowledge's sake were the order of the day for women, and courtesy books of the period stress 'prudence', 'delicacy' and 'propriety' as the means by which a woman should go about seeking in a lifelong mate. As an essayist called the Female Rambler points out in *The Lady's Magazine* of 1770, 'She who, intoxicated with flattery, protracts the triumphs of her beauty in youth, may live to lament the barren spoils of it in age. The hours of real courtship are so few and transitory, that they should be well-husbanded by her that would be a happy wife.'

Although finding a husband was paramount, there were more years for it than our impression of the era gives. As Jane Austen points out in *Persuasion*: 'It sometimes happens, that a woman is handsomer at twenty-nine than she was ten years before', although the more years a woman remained at home without a husband, the more she drained the finances of her family. At the beginning of the Georgian era, the notion that women were not innately sexual beings unless corrupted by men had come to the fore. So while women were invited to reply to personal ads, they did not regularly place their own, or not at least without desperation. Meanwhile, the men that placed the ads were regarded as fortune-hunters. One Sir John Dinseley even took to handing out flyers to find himself a wife; it took him fifteen years. By the end of the eighteenth century there were people ready to do the hunting for you (and with a promise of a faster return) in the form of marriage brokers, and marriage societies such as the New Matrimonial Plan provided a helpful grading system by which you could figure out if the broad-shouldered yet slightly stout gentleman in the naval uniform was suitably well born enough for your very well-read, very pretty (if slightly freckled) sister. Dating in and of itself was not, of course, a leisurely pursuit but a means of securing a good marriage. And a good marriage wasn't only one whereby the couple fell into a passionate heap after a solid game of bridge every night but one where status and money were secured for the couple. If you were very lucky, you got all of it: status, money, and a gaming partner with the stamina of a Vegas poker champ.

Making a good match was no less important for a working man. As an essay published in Volume 1 of *The Lady's Magazine*, which appeared in 1770, notes, 'Courtship is sure to be either the ruin or happy settling of every young tradesman who engages in it; if the choice be imprudent, it is ruin, whether it succeeds or not, and even where it is irreproachable, the time lost about it, and the neglect of business it occasions, are not easily made up to a young man.'

Contrary to the courtesy manuals of the Renaissance or the seventeenth century, which were all about men perfecting the art of flattery and getting underneath a lady's petticoats by way of a winning line, Regency suitors were encouraged to appeal to women's sense rather than their sensibility: 'During the smiling days of courtship,' writes Frances Friendly in *The Lady's Magazine*, addressing a male readership, 'avoid all the foolish flights of romance, and address your fair favourites as reasonable beings. Avoid flattery: a woman of sense will esteem you the more for it.'

Physically speaking, the ideal Regency gentleman was tall with a fine head of hair, a slim waist and buff chest – given that CrossFit wasn't on the cards, men were even known to wear corsets to achieve the right body shape. As with women though, a defective personality could ruin an otherwise admirable countenance. In a letter from the journalist and politician John Wilkes to a noble lord in London, dated 1764, Wilkes imagines the worst slander that can be slung at a man: 'He is the vilest wretch that Heaven ever suffered to exist – A Spendthrift! – A Gambler! – A Whoremonger! – Cheat! – Thief! And Vagabond!' There's that mention of money again.

Similarly, in *Pride and Prejudice*, for example, Mr Darcy starts out 'quite young, wonderfully handsome, extremely agreeable', only to become 'the proudest, most disagreeable man in the world' after he refuses to dance with Elizabeth Bennet at the Assembly ball. Later still, he admits that his pride, conceit and selfishness got in the way of his manners, in contrast with the demeanour of 'fairest, loveliest Elizabeth'. Women were regarded as the fairer sex, after all, and the idea that the love of a good one could redeem an undeserving man was beginning to take hold.

Still, if you didn't fancy using a Lonely Heart to secure an upstanding gentleman – and let's face it, after the 'Red Barn murder' of 1828 by which a man named William Corder lured, seduced and killed a twenty-something woman called Maria Marten by advertisement, only the desperate did – there was always the more traditional route of attending a ball or other public event. Women couldn't attend the theatre, a dance, or dinner without a chaperone, so balls were one of the few guaranteed opportunities for flirtation. Although still under the watchful gaze of an elder, here were a few hours where you could also make eyes at a potential partner, giving them a closer, face-to-face examination, as you took your positions opposite one another in a dance.

Rich families invested large sums of money to give their daughters a 'season' in London, which ran from March to June. Coming 'out' was crucial if you wanted the opportunity to find a rich husband. But it was also paramount that a woman didn't reveal her 'game'. The most desirable location at which to find a husband was an exclusive club called Almack's, also known as the 'Marriage Mart'. But getting a pass was tougher than finding a table at the Chiltern Firehouse – you needed to be gifted a voucher by one of seven noble patronesses. They were draconian doorwomen and would turn away anyone, however prominent, if they happened to be wrongly attired (the Duke of Wellington who once turned up in black trousers instead of regulation knee-breeches was a case in point). Conversation was strictly limited to pleasantries and mild gossip, and only debutantes with permission from a patroness could waltz – a permission given according to the grace of the dancer.

What you wore mattered. The Regency period was the beginning of a golden age of men's tailoring and being interested in fashion for fashion's sake became a legitimate hobby for women. What was even more significant for dating was the relatively skimpy quality of the new Grecian style of dress for the ladies. Arms and bosoms were bared and fabric skimmed the body, causing the octogenarian Lady Anne Barnard to remark at a dinner party, 'Who is that very handsome naked woman?' Corsets were out temporarily although a skintight undergarment designed to give a smooth line – essentially Regency shape-wear – didn't necessarily make for greater comfort, just more opportunity to show off one's natural curves. Of course, the empire-line fitting had the effect of making pretty much all women look pregnant, which in evolutionary terms one would have thought would have either attracted or repelled various men, depending on whether they found themselves reminded of the possibility of fertility, or of pre-existing up-the-duffery. Oriental and Indian shawls were added for warmth, and jewellery, hats, bonnets and other trimmings went in and out of fashion as rapidly as the latest debutantes.

Just as dress simplified, so did make-up. At the beginning of the eighteenth century it was fashionable to wear heavy white power and garish pops of blusher, but this soon gave way to a more natural look to match the rustic or classical style of the outfits. Rose, violet, peach and lily all featured in some of the more popular beauty products, while home-made remedies, such as green pineapple or onion juice to fend off wrinkles, and a breadcrumb and egg-white face mask, were affordable concoctions. Meanwhile a diet and exercise regime of a three-mile morning walk followed by steak and ale for breakfast sounds like a Georgian-style Atkins regime.

Men were just as well decked. Abandoning the wigs, knee breeches, and long surcoats of the earlier eighteenth century, they favoured long trousers, plain top boots and simple, form-fitting coats. There was, however, the Dandy, a man nearly entirely preoccupied with flamboyant style. Some of the more romantically inclined even tore their clothes with glass before stepping out to get that hot artistic hobo look. If anything, dating a dandy required patience: he was liable to take far more time getting ready than his female partner. Men also used a plethora of cosmetics, including powder, scent and oil in their hair, which they probably needed, given that they didn't wash it.

When it came to the socially acceptable rituals of dating, or courtship, leading to marriage, they were heavily proscribed. In fact, they were not even recognised as courtship at this stage. Men and women needed to be formerly introduced to one another in order to talk or dance and never called each other by their first names. Women needed to be 'out' in order to reply to men (only when approached first, of course), otherwise they could only speak when asked a question by a family member, and in theory, the older daughters of a family needed to be married off before the younger ones could enter the flirtation game. And at all times, whether at a ball or on a country walk, if there was a notable gentleman present, women needed to be accompanied by a chaperone, which was frequently their mother.

Still, a ball did give a real opportunity for interaction with the opposite sex even if it was frustratingly regimented. Women had to dance with everyone who asked them, or else no one – you could not demonstrate preference over dance partners. Unmarried men and women were not permitted to dance together for more than two sets, and only touched through gloved hands. Even handshakes were out of the question. Basically, you could expect about as much contact as at your junior school leavers disco. On the other hand, those who were already officially entangled experienced far greater thrills. Was your partner's dance with another lady as innocent as he intimated? With the help of a so-called 'jealousy glass' – a mini telescope with a mirror built into the left or right – you could keep a side-eye on his flirtations off the dance floor.

For everyone, male and female alike, there was the additional help of fan language. The original fanology, published in 1797, set out a code of conversation by flutter, and full instructions on how to hold and move a fan to the required effect. Below are some of the not-so-secret expressions.

Letting the fan rest on the right cheek – 'Yes'
Letting the fan rest on the left cheek – 'No'
Dropping the fan – 'We will be friends'

Carrying an open fan in the left hand – 'Come and talk to me'

Fanning slowly – 'He liked it and so he put a ring on it' (I am married)

Fanning quickly – 'I am engaged'

Opening a fan wide – 'Wait for me'

A half-closed fan pressed to the lips – 'You may kiss me'

Twirling the fan in the right hand – 'I love another'

Twirling the fan in the left hand – 'We are being watched'

Placing a closed fan on the right eye – 'When can I see you?'

Shutting a fully open fan slowly – 'I promise to marry you'

Drawing the fan across the eyes – 'I am sorry'

Placing your fan near your heart – 'I love you'

Rather like the scene in *Four Weddings and a Funeral* where a wedding guest tries to impress Hugh Grant's dishy, deaf on-screen brother with her newly acquired, ropey sign language, you can imagine a young novice accidentally confusing the left with the right, fanning love for someone else when they mean to merely put others off the scent of their flirtation, or cursing if they dropped a fan while aiming for a 'wait' gesture.

In fact, for the unattached, the thrill was all in the possibilities. When it came to alerting the person you were interested in of your feelings, outside of fan language, you had few options. No gifts were to be exchanged under any circumstances and correspondence was not to be entered into at this preliminary stage – hence why Lonely Hearts ads, when they appeared, were deemed so risqué. And the gentleman was to make all of the advances. Mutual feeling and love matches were encouraged, but there was a rulebook for the unfolding of the potential relationship. This extract from Jane Austen's *Persuasion* sums up the formula: 'They were gradually acquainted, and when acquainted, rapidly and deeply in love. It would be difficult to say which had seen highest perfection in the other, or which has been the happiest; she, in receiving his declarations and proposals, or he in having them accepted.'

The following two letters, taken from the *London Universal Letter-writer*, published in 1809, demonstrate perfectly the delicate overtures made for the hand of a lady.

In the first, the young woman in question – let's call her Eveline – alerts her father to a potential suitor named Smith who, in a rather roundabout way, 'has made some overtures to my cousin Arnold, in the way of courtship to me'.

To her suitor's credit, 'Eveline' explains to her father, that her cousin 'has a high opinion of him [the suitor] and his circumstances'. She goes on to list his professional successes – 'He has been set up three years, possesses a very good business, and lives in credit and fashion. He is about twenty-seven years old, and is likely in his person. He seems not to want sense nor manners, and is come of a good family'.

But even though 'He has broken his mind to me, and boasts how well he can maintain me' Eveline is at pains to reassure her father that she's given him 'no encourage-ment', and yet 'he resolves to persevere, and pretends extraordinary affection and esteem'. In other words, Papa

Don't Preach – I'm not in trouble and I don't intend to be any time soon.

In the same letter-writing manual, there appears a model suitor's letter – let's call him Gerald – hypothetically addressed to a potential new father-in-law, which begins with the very cautious address, 'Sir,—THOUGH personally unknown to you, I take the liberty to declare the great value and affection I have for your amiable daughter, whom I have had the honor to see at my friend's house. I should think myself entirely unworthy of her favour, and of your approbation, if I could have thought of influencing her resolution, but in obedience to your pleasure'.

Phew. Talk about going round the country houses. Going on to assure his potential father-in-law that he comes from good stock, while setting out his upstanding professional credentials, including a frank confession of his finances ('I had a thousand pounds to begin with, which I have improved to fifteen hundred'), and his intentions to expand the business, Gerald finishes by saying in a very roundabout way that he hopes the potential father-in-law will grant him the 'greatest happiness of my life' by allowing him to marry his daughter – even though his balls are so tight in his breeches he doesn't even mention the 'M' word anywhere in his fawning treatise.

You can see how important it was to stress not only virtue of character but voluptuousness of bank account. However, if parents were not enamoured with the match, a father did not have to confirm the hand of his daughter. As so happens in *Persuasion*, 'Sir Walter, on being applied to, without actually withholding his consent, or saying it should never be, gave it all the negative of great

11

astonishment, great coldness, great silence, and a professed resolution of doing nothing for his daughter.'

But if the family was in favour, and a proposal of marriage was accepted, official 'courtship' began, prior to the planning of a wedding. Although couples still required a chaperone at this stage, they were now able to converse privately, sit together, exchange gifts, even touch a few gloved fingers in greeting.

While the legal age for marriage was twenty-one in England and Wales, many women were married between the ages of seventeen and twenty (which was allowed as long as a parent didn't explicitly forbid it). The 'settlement' outlined the financial details of the marriage, and included the dowry amount, how much the woman was to receive in 'pin money' (i.e. her allowance for clothes, hobbies etc.), what her children should inherit, and what her financial circumstance would be after her husband's death, known as the 'jointure'. Given that most Georgian women had no means of their own, it was vital that the details of her future financial life be outlined in this way.

Ensuring the longevity of a marriage was so important that 1753 saw the introduction of the Marriage Act, a piece of legislation designed to put a stop to 'Fleet marriages'. Until 1753, English law merely required couples to say their vows in front of an ordained clergyman. Given that the clergyman didn't need to be in charge of a parish, this gave bigamists and those whose marriage would scandalise the local community the opportunity to wed in secret. At the Fleet prison in London, home to convict clergy who had debt issues, there were numerous ordained priests willing to do the dirty nuptial deed for a minimal fee. When the Marriage Act, also known as the Hardwicke Act, came into force, couples wishing to marry were required to have the banns read in church, or to obtain a special licence from the local bishop or Archbishop of Canterbury.

In order to ensure that couples did not use it as merely a way to cover up a prior marriage or other scandal, this licence required a £100 bond to be forfeited in the event of something untoward being revealed. Mainly used by the aristocracy or those in the public eye, the licence then followed the same requirements as the banns – that there be a seven-day 'cooling off' period between procuring permission to marry and the wedding taking place; that the couple had to be married between 8 a.m. and noon, and that the parish in which the wedding was to take place was named somewhere along the way – either in the licence, or by nature of the banns being read in the parish church prior to the ceremony.

Roman Catholics could be married in a Catholic church but the marriage was only sanctified once the ceremony had also been officiated by a Church of England priest. The only people exempt from the rules were Quakers and Jews, although both members of the couple had to be one or the other in order to qualify.

It was because of these new restrictions that couples who did not meet the criteria began to elope to Gretna Green, the first place across the English border where Scottish marriage laws remained more liberal, in particular where those under twenty-one could marry without parental approval. These marriages were frequently love matches where one or both partners had a precarious financial situation, or a mismatched social profile. Today, Gretna celebrates its history as a hasty wedding venue and makes a packet out of marketing itself as a one-stop marriage shop.

Counter-intuitively, a marriage didn't necessarily mean the end of one's 'dating' life. Given that divorce was nearly unthinkable and required a parliamentary act passing in order to grant it, being or having a mistress became socially acceptable, mainly because many members of the royal family, including King George III himself, had all taken mistresses and expected them to be treated with due civility. Becoming a mistress was also lucrative and one of the only ways for a woman to be truly financially independent. In fact, when the Duke of Clarence and a certain Mrs Jordon began their affair, the financial details of it were set out in the *Morning Post*. Top-notch mistresses could command as much as £100,000 a year. Harriette Wilson was the most successful mistress of the age, and along with her sister Fanny and their mutual friend Julia Johnstone, they were known as the Fashionable Impure. Wilson enmeshed dozens of dukes, dignitaries, and almost the Prince of Wales, before publishing her memoirs in an act of supreme kiss 'n' tell. Despite being full of candid gossip about her lovers, she managed to maintain her social status, probably because all the ones she hadn't mentioned feared being named and shamed. But while affairs between nobles and celebrity mistresses were public knowledge, and none the worse for it, affairs between lesser known contemporaries were to be strictly discreet. After all, common adultery could be the basis of a 'crim con', or criminal conversation detailing the misdeeds, which could then be used as evidence for divorce, something to be avoided at all costs.

Rather progressively, an affair wasn't always conceived as the woman's fault. As a writer called Frances Friendly mused in a 1770 edition of *The Lady's Magazine*, 'Can such husbands wonder at their wives seeking for pleasure and entertainment abroad? – Many do it too much I own, but many are drove to it, and do it very innocently.'

Aside from mistressing, there was also the option of becoming a fully fledged lady of the night. According to Dan Cruickshank's book, *The Secret History of Georgian London: How the Wages of Sin Shaped the Capital*, it's estimated that up to one in five women in mid-eighteenth-century London were embroiled in its sex industry. Being a high-class courtesan came with rich rewards, not dissimilar from being a mistress; the ability to rent a fancy new property in one of the fashionable parts of town such as Marylebone, for example; the choicest outfits; the best dining experiences and trips to the opera. The most famous high-class call girl of her age, Kitty Fisher, commanded a fee of a hundred guineas a night, the equivalent of more than £1000 in today's money. With amounts like that on offer, why bother with a husband?

But for the majority, spouse-hunting still took up an inordinate amount of time. As the nineteenth century wore on and romantic literature flourished, so did the fascination with romantic love. Finding your happy-ever-after match was about to become more than a mere social chore.

Chapter Two

The Early Victorian era:
Taking the tussie-mussie

When Queen Victoria and Prince Albert were married in 1840, theirs was a radical union. Firstly, rather than waiting for him to pop the question, Victoria had sidestepped the fact it wasn't a leap year and asked Albert to marry her, which I suppose makes her something of a historical hersband. Secondly, they were madly in love (or at least so was Queen Victoria) and everybody had to know about it.

'Oh, to feel I was and am loved by such an Angel as Albert was too great a delight to describe,' wrote Queen Victoria upon their engagement. 'He is perfection. Oh, how I love and adore him, I cannot say!'

So the bar for her subjects' marriages was set. Love – chest-swelling, cheek-rouging, pulse-pumping, teeth-grinding fervour – was not only fashionable, but royally sanctioned.

The notion that the Victorians were all chair-leg covering prudes, afraid their crinolines might rustle the word 'sex' is about as accurate as suggesting that all of us in the Nowties are potential contestants for C4's *Naked Attraction*. As industrialisation brought increased sexual freedom, anxieties about sex duly increased. But rather than silencing the Victorians, this had the opposite effect, and soon sex, relationships and romance had never been discussed more openly. Whether it was believing that women needed an orgasm in order to conceive, or the fear that masturbation caused disease, every aspect of sexuality was scrutinised and debated. Love, however, remained the watchword: as marital advisor John Maynard wrote in 1866: 'Rather refuse the offers of a hundred men than marry one you do not, cannot love.'

For a woman, the pursuit of love above all else was certainly a noble cause: 'when a woman loves a man so much she is ready to give up friends, position and comfort for his sake; she is worthy of all commendation, for she proves herself high-souled and magnanimous'. And yet exercising prudence was still advised: 'ladies and gentlemen, if they are determined to make a sacrifice, [to] be quite sure that the object is worthy of it, as lifelong regret not unfrequently follows a so-called romantic marriage'. Good women were not presumed to be sexual, an opinion confirmed by physician William Acton: 'The majority of women (happily for them) are not very much troubled by sexual feeling of any kind' and so romantic desire retained an innately chaste quality. And as 1897's *Manners for Men* warned, 'Should marriage follow upon such courtship [. . .] where the girl takes the initiative, the union is very seldom a happy one.'

If a couple had exercised due decorum, and not merely followed Queen Victoria's breeches-busting example, an engagement could take up to five years, mainly because the middle and upper working classes had to save up for married life. While gentlemen were no longer required to approach a potential bride's father for her hand, as *The Lover's Guide to Courtship and Marriage* of 1885 put it,

'. . . gentlemen, Be sure that you can afford a wife before you determine to take one . . . Better wait for ten years than marry before you can afford it.'

Meanwhile, young women of the upper middle and upper classes still 'came out' anywhere between the ages of sixteen and eighteen. Despite the Royal 'Wheeee!' the function of marriage for them was still based on considerations of social mobility rather than romantic ones. For debutantes, the transition to womanhood was marked by letting one's dress down, putting one's white-feather-decorated hair up, and rolling up at a royal ball to curtsy before, and kiss the hand of Queen Victoria. Backing out of the room without tripping over your virginal frock sealed the debutante deal and then you were free to pack in as many dances with eligible bachelors as the night allowed. Girls spent two to four seasons husband-hunting before they were considered 'spent'. At that point they had to hope a sudden illness struck a distant relative who had the foresight to leave them a massively generous annual income, or that one of the young men they'd danced with several seasons before came to his amoeba-slow senses and appeared with more than a posy.

Across the classes, courtesy manuals were still consulted but with less commitment and respect, with much dating advice being treated as humorous or satirical entertainment. *The Etiquette of Love, Courtship and Marriage*, published in 1847, was one of the go-to manuals of the age, keen to explain the inequities of class and gender when it came to marriage: 'a lady of high rank does not raise her husband to the same position as she formerly occupied; but sinks down to his standard; but the gentleman raises the lady, however much below himself, to the same position in society'.

Such manuals also offered advice on that perennial question – the age gap. Take this from the same title published in 1865 – to calculate the best age difference 'most conducive to happiness', 'halve the man's age and then add seven to the remainder'. This meant a guy at thirty was best suited to a twenty-two-year-old girl, and a guy of forty, a twenty-seven-year-old. There was also this advice on finding out a lady's age when you were sure she had subtracted a few years: 'Tell her to put down the number of the month in which she was born then to multiply it by 2, then to add 5, then to multiply it by 50 then to add her age, then to subtract 365, then to add 115, then tell her the amount she has left. The two figures at the right will be her age, and the remainder the month of her birth . . . Try it.'

The difficulties of ascertaining her age were just the beginning of a gentleman's tribulations. Take the ritual of a house call. To begin with, the Victorians used calling cards. Rather like today's personalised business cards, only without the Twitter handle and endless blog/Insta listings framed onto a background pic of your last long-haul holiday, they were decorated with a name and artistic design, and were first dropped off by potential guests or suitors at the home of the hosts they wished to visit and left with the servants. If a visit was agreeable, a host would signal this by sending one of their own cards. Young ladies used their mother's calling cards, and received those of prospective suitors on a tray. They then had the power to return the cards or not – perhaps the single most important power-move afforded to women during the entire courtship process, apart from out and out refusal. In fact, the complex etiquette of calling cards is set out in Mrs Humphrey's *Manners for Men*, an etiquette guide of 1897, with an entire section dedicated to their exchange and placement.

If a gentleman was welcome, he still could not directly call on a young lady. Instead, he had to visit whichever respectable female relative with whom she was living at the time. She could be present, but only under the auspices of her guardian. Even up until the end of the nineteenth century, the rules about how he should appear were exceedingly precise. Take this from 'Practical Etiquette', dated 1899:

> In making an evening call a man should appear about half past eight, and remain an hour. Even if his visit is to the daughter; he should ask for her mother. When a young man is paying a visit, and the older members of the family are in the room, he should, in leaving, bid them good-night first, and afterward say his farewell to the young girl on whom he has called. It is in bad taste for her to go any further than the parlour door.

As well as 'the call', gentlemen could be invited to other family events, such as a tea party, an 'at-home' (whereby guests gathered for music, tea and dessert between 4 and 7 p.m.), a reception, a dinner party, (described by *Manners for Men* as 'an institution sacred to the highest rites of hospitality') or an intelligent conversation or private 'theatricals'. Sometimes it was even just for a game of charades.

In particular, 'theatricals' gave young women a chance to dress up and to act out love scenes with the attendant young men. The piano also offered an opportunity for more discreet flirtation. She might showcase her sweet singing voice while he turned her pages. Or there was even the euphemistic opportunity to duet together. In the summer, picnics and croquet were the most popular dating-style entertainments. Balls, meanwhile, retained all their allure – and their restrictions, such as not being able to dance with anyone if you refused a certain gentleman, remained.

Manners, as ever, in these situations were scrupulously dictated. Ideal men were imagined as: 'Reliable as rocks, judicious in every action, dependable in trifles as well as the large affairs of life, full of mercy and kindness to others, affectionate and well-loved in their homes, their lives are pure and kindly [. . .] And he must have a sense of humour too.'

Etiquette between the sexes on the streets was just as important as in the drawing room: 'In crowded streets he may often have to fall behind, but he should never allow anyone to interpose between her and him. Should the pressure from the crowd become extreme, his duty is to protect her from it as much as possible, but never by putting his arm round her waist. A hand on either side of the lady's shoulders is usually sufficient.'

Even a simple introduction was fraught: 'It must always be borne in mind that the assumption of a woman's social superiority lies at the root of these rules of conduct. It is bad manners to introduce people without permission.' And the golden rule? 'Never introduce a lady to gentleman; but always the gentleman to the lady.'

But while gentlemen were encouraged to kowtow to a lady's social superiority, this was only in the cases where she truly was a lady: 'A young man once asked me if it would be etiquette to offer an unknown lady an umbrella in the street, supposing she stood in need of one. I replied:

"No lady would accept the offer from a stranger, and the other sort of person might never return the umbrella." '

What a well-bred lady could accept, however, was a Valentine's card. Valentine's cards had first been sent in the fifteenth century, but the availability of cheap paper combined with new printing techniques meant they were easier than ever before to produce, and the first commercial printing of Valentine's cards began in the early nineteenth century. Whether it was the most affordable cards featuring simple woodcut illustrations at 6 pence, or the more expensive varieties featuring lace, ribbons and gems at several shillings, the trend for sending the cards, which were usually left unsigned, or most, initialled, spread like wildfire. In 1836, sixty thousand Valentine's cards were sent, and after the introduction of the Penny Post in 1840, this rose to more than four hundred thousand. By 1871, the number had more than tripled again. The Valentine's card ignited Victorians' passions as much as decorating their homes.

Between 1830 and 1860, intricate lace paper Valentine's cards were all the rage and Rimmel (father of the cosmetic company) collaborated with artists to produce scented cards. And then there was the trend for 'vinegar valentines', a deliberately insulting or particularly rude card you sent to someone you either didn't like, wanted to put off, or wanted to warn about something – the infidelity of their fiancé, for example. In 1850, it was fashionable to sell paper currency or cheques, entitling the recipient to '1000 kisses', for example. These cheques were so popular – and simultaneously so frowned upon by the government – that they were even banned in certain cities.

The Victorians were also enamoured with floriography, or sending messages by flowers. Depending on the bouquet depicted on the card you received – or the real bunch – you could decode messages about your lover's feelings for you. Daffodils signalled new beginnings, daisies innocence, and lilacs meant the first emotions of love, and dictionaries unpacking the symbolism became popular. Flowers were one of the most common gift brought to parties or when visiting so special attention was given to what you conveyed with them. And then there were 'tussie-mussies' or nose-gays – bunches of scented herbs with a single flower in the centre, initially used to disguise the unsavoury smells of Victorian England, but frequently given as tokens of affection. Rather like fans, one could ascertain just how much the recipient loved you depending on where the recipient held them next to on the body.

As the post took off, so did letter-writing and the manuals that guided writers as to just which sentences to string together became even more popular than they had been in the Regency. Given that women had been consumers of these guides for so many years, they were thought to have had the most practise in perfecting the ideal tone – for once, it was women who were expected to exercise 'reason' rather than men. However, letter-writing manuals encouraged all users to be discreet – avoiding social embarrassment mattered to the Victorians just about more than establishing the working week, contacting their dead relatives at a séance, and figuring out the identity of Jack the Ripper put together. Engaged couples were allowed to express affection, however; *The Letter Writer for Lovers*, published in 1878, advised 'If the engaged couple are really loving and wish to express their feelings in loving phrases, let them by all means do so; but let this be done in a gentlemanlike and ladylike manner.'

Where you put the stamp also gave out a romantic message. According to *Reeves Pocket Companion* of 1886, a stamp placed upside down on the left-hand corner of the envelope signified 'I love you', while one placed the right way up in the top right-hand corner meant only, 'I wish your friendship'. Upside down on the right-hand corner was even more damning – 'Write no more'.

Given that courtship was seen very much as a trial period, women were encouraged to test out their potential husbands for evidence of ill feeling towards their families, 'foppish' behaviour, or slovenly habits. They were also advised to be prudent: 'Do not fall hopelessly in love with the first man that pays attention to you,' is the advice from *The Lover's Guide* of 1885.

Once engaged, there was a tight code governing how the couple might behave in public. They were urged not to show off their status, for example. For a woman, according to *The Lover's Guide* of 1885, 'a lady should conduct herself almost as though she were already married; all other suitors, if she possessed more than the one she has already accepted, should be made thoroughly to understand, for once and for all, that she can no longer accept their attentions'.

An engagement ring could help. Diamonds were not yet on the horizon, but rings set with stones that spelled out the name of the lover by corresponding gem to letter were. Alongside a ring, 'jewellery, a bouquet, a fan, a locket' were also all allowed, 'but no dresses or other necessary articles, unless as in the olden time, a camel's hair shawl, now entirely out of fashion', so pronounceth the *Correct Social Usage* of 1903.

Given that engagements could last so long, they were in some ways high-risk ventures – particularly if your partner were to pull out on you, four years in. For a woman, that was four fertile years wasted, and maybe another four years ahead of you to sit out another engagement. Old Maidenhood beckoned while your feckless fiancé fannied about.

So to remedy the situation, women started to bring breach-of-promise suits. These were legal cases for damages designed to provide financial compensation for the slight of being jilted.

Eight hundred and seventy-five were brought before the English courts between 1750 and 1950, nearly all of them by women, and by those of the lower middle and upper working classes. For women with modest means, they were a godsend when their reputation and future domestic happiness lay in tatters. They could also protect a man's reputation if his fiancée appeared to be of less than a modest and chaste character than she'd led him to believe.

There were a few interesting defences. Firstly, in the case of a man being sued by a woman, the most popular thing to claim was that your fiancée was unchaste. You could also cite illness, immaturity (i.e. being under the age of twenty-one), or mental incapacity (which included being too drunk to remember a proposal).

There were some odd caveats though. If you were already married and your betrothed was already aware of the fact, breach of promise didn't hold.

How breach of promise was decided was complex. Letters formed evidence. Women who found themselves pregnant and applied for assistance at the London Foundling Hospital, for example, used correspondence detailing their relationships as proof that a betrothal had been promised and that they weren't prostitutes – unwed mothers could not claim. An inferred engagement could produce a claim – as in the case of one Amelia Rooke who claimed that her forty-year older cousin had made overtures to her – but the damages were limited (Rooke only received a farthing) and most judges exercised discretion. Pregnancy was actually seen as greater proof that a discussion about marriage had indeed taken place.

From 1850, claims for breach of promise increased significantly; the sly and impecunious had cottoned on to the fact that you only needed to produce one witness to your alleged marriage proposal for it to stick. At this time neither the plaintiff nor the defendant were allowed in the witness box; the idea was that the urge to lie would be too great, and that one or both of them would damn their immortal soul by doing so. When this changed, so did the quality of evidence given and the fraudulent claimsters began to shrivel away. But it also put off many working and middle class women who did not fancy having their morals scrutinised in the witness box. Upper class men and women, meanwhile, began to opt for private settlements.

Meanwhile, breach of promise still exists in the US today, and a recent case in 2013 saw a Georgia mother of four who'd given up work to raise her and her fiancé's children awarded $50,000 compensation after he broke off their engagement, a whole four years later.

The sentiment that buoyed breach of promise also paved the way for the Divorce Act of 1857, which ruled that women could sue for divorce if their husbands committed adultery and had either deserted them for two years or done them physical harm. Adultery with a relative, man or animal meant an automatic right to divorce.

Meanwhile, a husband could still seek divorce from his wife based on adultery alone but the new law went some way to giving women more rights in the event of marital breakdown, and by the end of the 1880s, women had a right to own their own property and custody of their children, whether they'd been unfaithful or not.

But ahead of divorce lay the option of refusal, in the event an unsuitable suitor made an unwanted proposal of marriage. In the 1879 edition of *The Worcester Letter Writer*, originally published in New York, there are multiple templates for refusing a suitor, depending on whether the problem is that he is unsteady, too young, or whether the object of his affections simply didn't return his feelings.

Meanwhile, chaperones continued to be used in the Victorian era, although they were either governesses or, frequently, paid older women who kept their younger charges in check on the street and at social gatherings. As a manual of 1899, called 'Chaperonage', has it, 'A chaperon is not to watch and to restrain her, but to certify that her bloom is unimpaired and to compel others to respect it.' Chaperones weren't out to prohibit sexual entanglements for prohibition's sake, but to avert scandal.

If chaperones had protected the modesty of scantily clad, milk-maid-alike Regency girls, Victorian dress did an even better job of enforcing their chastity. A typical Victorian lady wore a chemise, drawers, a corset, an under-petticoat, a hoop skirt or crinoline, an over-petticoat, a long-sleeved gown, and never left the house without bonnet and gloves. Drawers in particular were a new, modesty-preserving addition to a lady's attire, and their ability to keep a lady 'cool' of lust was facilitated by their baggy nature.

Even if you were left alone with your gentleman caller for more than five minutes, how was he going to negotiate all that fabric? As if social stigma wasn't reason enough for the well-to-do avoiding premarital sex.

On the other hand, if Victorian ladies' dress did not make for easy access, it certainly made for easy viewing. Take the crinoline – a stiff, hooped skirt that swung from side to side, tipped back, and afforded many an amorous man a generous knickerless view, given that drawers did not come into fashion until the 1870s. As the bawdy riddle of the day had it, 'Why may the crinoline be justly regarded as a social invention? Because it enables us to see more of our friends.'

The Victorians prized modesty just as the Georgians had, but there was an added element of sexual frisson. Nearly all women wore exceedingly low-cut evening gowns that stopped just short of revealing the nipples, regardless of age. Many lotions and potions were recommended for the firming, toning and enlarging of breasts. Although as one nineteenth-century etiquette author had it, 'No good can come of such methods ... the only legitimate procedure to alter the figure is bust padding, though it must be said that it might be considered a rather cruel deception by some women and directed towards the other sex.' The ideal Victorian figure was slimmer than it had been in the Regency era. Between 1881 and 1900, the average corseted waist was twenty-two inches – an inch smaller than the previous decade. Expert advice also now emphasised protecting youthful skin and a girlish figure. Still, Victorian porn, as today, favoured a more voluptuous figure and countless journals of the time make reference to a preference for ample thighs, bottoms and bosoms. Men's bodies were also ripe for the objectifying, and the emphasis on muscles in contemporary newspaper accounts of notable sportsmen of the day creates a parallel with the love of an exposed cleavage. And then there was the Victorian trend for physiognomy, the belief that you could glean knowledge of people's personalities through their body parts. As Victorian social historian Fern Riddell has pointed out, full lips were favoured in both sexes as proof as amorosity, as were larger feet for proof of stability – 'small-footed persons are dangerously prone to gaiety and evolutions across the ballroom'. Similarly, women with small, long necks 'will not make ardent lovers and are commonly far more amiable and affectionate than given to passionate embracing'. Overall, it was recommended somebody with contrasting body parts, taller or shorter, thinner or fatter, fairer or darker, as this would create ' *"the union of a soul within a soul"* '.

Just as the Victorians enjoyed the secret language of flowers, so did they employ euphemisms in other kinds of decoration. Take the pearl, a mainstay of Victorian jewellery – which was a euphemism for the clitoris, and which was often worn in a long string draped in the bare cleavage of an evening gown; it certainly brings a whole new meaning to the term 'pearl necklace'.

As for the idea that the Victorians covered the legs of tables and chairs lest they be reminded of their own body parts, this apparently was more the practice in America, and reported back by bemused English travellers who came into contact with it. At any rate, Victorian ladies did sometimes show off more than a buttoned boot and silk-stocking-clad ankle; if they were attending a fancy dress party, they might don a fairy outfit and flash a full limb, and at the beach, the accepted swimming attire was either skirt and bloomers, or, more commonly, skirt and stockings. Until the 1870s, nude bathing was actually more common, and although men and women bathed separately, their beaches frequently nestled next to one another, affording anyone with a telescope or binoculars a hard-core eyeful.

Meanwhile, working-class women may have been toiling away in the factories and mills of England, but they had more freedom than their middle- and upper-class counter-parts when it came to sex and courtship. For a start, they left the house each day and, if they did not walk, took public transport alongside men to their workplaces, which gave them ample opportunities to meet potential suitors. The opportunities for meeting at entertainment venues were greater too; of course, there was no 'season' if you were a factory worker, but there was church, music halls, museums and the theatre, where you might get even more opportunity to get your flirt on.

In particular, the music hall, the most popular entertain-ment venue of the nineteenth century, was one of the best venues at which to meet a love match. All the best ingredi-ents of today's strip clubs were there: alcohol, music, scant-ily clad performers and attendees, and an atmosphere of off-the-clock revelry. In fact, a petition led by the Temperance movement in Glasgow against the Whitebait Music Hall cited young women 'so scantily clothed as to be almost naked dancing upon stages before crowds of men, sitting drinking beer and spirits, and smoking cigars and pipes, while men sang songs both blasphemous and filthy, containing, as they did, suggestions of a coarse and inde-cent nature'. Similarly, Bradford town clerk Mr Mossman denied a local pub's application for dance evenings by saying that it was too near to a cheap lodging house opposite, 'where invitations, seductions and allurements to wrong were hold out to young people'.

Originally not the preserve of women, this had changed when the Canterbury Music Hall opened in 1852 in Lambeth, London and introduced the concept of Ladies Night on a Thursday. The brainchild of owner Charles Morton, who thought it would civilise the men, Ladies Thursday in fact turned out to have the opposite effect, and soon the gentlemen in attendance were appearing with anybody *but* their wives and fiancées. What had begun as an attempt to celebrate Thursday as prime 'date night' had turned into a full-on infidelity club.

Even in London though, suspicions ran high of women who visited music halls by themselves, the presumption being that they were almost certainly prostitutes, and in 1885 the National Vigilance Association organised a campaign to raise the standards of social morality, repressing sexuality and praising chastity, which directly targeted the music halls. But despite protestations, halls thrived and, by the end of the nineteenth century, there were over three hundred licensed halls in London alone.

Still, many working class couples at the music halls and other venues did 'keep company' and that included having premarital sex. It's thought that between one- and two-fifths of all working-class women were pregnant on marriage. By the mid-1700s, most American and English working-class brides had already had sex before marriage, and while the Marriage Act of 1753 had formerly prohibited all sexual relations until after the ceremony, it's clear that it did little to dissuade people – it was almost impossible to police, for a start. Letters shared between lovers, parish records and the number of illegitimate children born do all give us the evidence, although by the 1840s there was some knowledge of the rhythm method of birth control. Finding a place to have sex in the days of shared quarters could be tricky; Sundays out in the countryside or the back of a hansom cab might make do for a bed, but whether it was a servant's attic room, or the kitchen floor, people also found their opportunities to utilise a horizontal surface when masters and mistresses left the premises.

In fact, when many a mistress went out, a woman in service could find herself the recipient of her master's affections, wanted or otherwise. The scarcity of contraception, fear of STIs, maternal mortality rate and the fact the number of female servants rose by 33 per cent between 1851 and 1884 meant that men with leverage all too frequently got their sexual kicks with the women that worked for them. Female servants were seen by many as free prostitutes.

Curiously, working-class women were often more secretive about their relationships, partly because those in service were forbidden from having 'followers', but also it seems because many didn't think there was any point in revealing them to friends until it had reached the stage of pending marriage. This could backfire though if the gentleman they were dating turned out not to be anything of the sort. Mothers admitted to London's Foundling Hospital with a child they could not support revealed that most of their pregnancies were due not to one-day/afternoon/night stands, but to ongoing relationships, with three-quarters of them lasting six months or longer. Time and again, the women would cite 'the promise of marriage' as the reason they had agreed to sex. Many men also promised to marry the girls even after they found out they were pregnant, only to go back on their word later. Interestingly, country mores were somewhat different. If a young, single girl found herself pregnant, her family would frequently actively prevent marriage with the father of the child, even in the event he proposed to make an honest woman out of her, in order that they benefit from the income she brought to the family through working.

Still, not everyone went all the way. The Poor Law Amendment Act in 1834 imposed penalties for women with illegitimate children and so 'bundling', an intimate but fully clothed method of petting, cuddling and courtship, once common in rural areas, spread to the rapidly urbanising cities.

By the end of the century, the Victorians had got themselves into a complete state about sex. While pornography and prostitution flourished, attempts to clean up the streets of fallen women and deal with women's emotional 'hysteria' via mechanical devices were flourishing. Masturbation remained the greatest sin, as damaging to men as it was to women, although there were additional warnings given to the fairer sex: 'Its indulgence will ruin the health, cause nervous disease, and destroy taste for healthy matrimonial intercourse by blunting the finer sexual feelings' (from *The Wife's Handbook*, Dr Henry Arthur Allbutt, 1886).

But vibrators were the least of their worries. It was the debate around women's rights that was about to rock the domestic boat.

Chapter Three

The late Victorian era:
Ladies who chap-chat

When the Married Women's Property Act came in in 1870, it set about upending a balance of power and so subtly altered the courtship dynamic ever after. Up until 1870, whatever a woman had inherited and owned became her husband's upon marriage. Now, an heiress could retain her inherited lands and houses when she said 'I do', which put something of a dampener on a certain kind of cad's fortune-hunting. It also put to an end the need for dowries, pin money and allowances when a woman entered marriage with her own wealth. This meant that marrying for love became even more viable amongst the elite. The law had ruled in love's favour.

Meanwhile, there was an additional conversation going on about whether women should marry at all. The 'free lovers' of the late nineteenth century wanted to revolution-ise relationships. Contrary to what the name conjures, they weren't preaching the shagadelic message of 1960s hippies, but rather arguing that women be afforded more sexual satisfaction in their personal relationships if freed of the assumption that women were best served by marriage and children. As the anarchist Lillie White announced in 1891, 'When women learn that their best and highest object in life is to be independent and free, instead of living to make some man comfortable; when she finds out that she must first be happy herself to make others happy, we shall have loving, harmonious families and happy homes.'

Given that many women were having unprotected sex, the free love movement also wanted to protect them against what they called 'enforced motherhood'. Initially, this didn't mean supporting contraception but other ways of having sexual relations – the 'Dianaism' concept, for example, which stressed non-penetrative sexual activity. Eventually, the debate around contraception grew so strong that its use was inevitable. But it would be another twenty years before a scientist specialising in coal and seed ferns called Marie Stopes would revolutionise public thinking. In the meantime, a woman called Annie Besant would be tried for obscenity for publishing a pamphlet on contraception. Still, there was a thirst for the contraband information; the pamphlet in question, *The Law of Population*, published in 1877, had sold 175,000 copies by 1891.

Women's increased freedom in public spaces was also challenging previously held etiquette about how they should behave in the presence of men. Take this from 1897's *Manners for Men*, on the subject of going Dutch at dinnertime: 'A really well-bred girl or woman would make it clear that she intended to pay for her own meal, and that only on that condition would she accept the escort of the young man.'

Similarly, if there's something else that affected dating more greatly than in any other era, it was transport and there were two modes in particular – the steam train and the bicycle – that revolutionised the possibilities for romance. By 1852, there were 6600 miles of railway in England and Scotland, with 507 million tickets purchased by 1871. Everybody, bar shepherds and farmers emotionally hog-tied to their livestock, travelled by rail, and there were two main ways it hotted things up – firstly, it meant you could now travel and see a lover in a different town or even county, and secondly, it placed men and women in a novel proximity, situated as they were in the close confinement of narrow carriages and dimly lit waiting rooms.

There were ladies-only waiting rooms and carriages, but women frequently did not stick to them, or else visited the smoking carriages, and there was soon a moral panic about women's safety, which seems really to be a sexist reaction to women's increasing freedom. Men worried that they would be accused of rape: 'gentlemen passengers, as well as railway officers of all classes, constantly refuse to travel singly with a stranger of the weaker sex, under the belief that it is only common prudence to avoid in this manner all risk of being accused, for purposes of extortion, of insult, or assault' was the conclusion of one Captain Tyler, reporting from the Board of Trade to the railway companies in 1864.

There were even pornographic novels about the situation, including one entitled *Raped on the Railway*, although actual attacks were few and far between. The message, though, was that the railway was a place of potential danger for women, and one in which they needed to exercise modesty and caution.

However, 1889's *Hints to Lady Travellers* offered women some advice for dealing in a dignified way with the railways. It recommends women buy themselves a set of railway keys so they aren't confined to being prisoners in their carriage, to enlist the protection of the train guard at the beginning of a journey, and to take care around luggage: 'I know a lady who narrowly escaped a broken neck by her husband's portmanteau falling upon her head from the luggage rack above'.

So it continues. In travelling, 'women may abuse the privileges too long withheld from them, in the first bewilderment of feeling a new power in their hands', and it goes on to conclude that 'none, perhaps is less open to abuse, and surely none is more excellent in itself and its results' than being allowed to venture forth.

As for bicycles, they were the weapon of the Victorian 'New Woman', that she-devilish creature of the late nineteenth century who drank, smoked, and wore bloomers to enable her to get her leg over and give up side saddle for good. Originally, the tricycle had been invented for women, designed so that they could ride in full skirt and thus preserve their modesty. Social custom around the tricycle also required that women ride with a chaperone, which put a bit of a dampener on what should have been a freedom-giver. But when the two-wheeler came out, women shrugged off the chaperone and adventured out on their own, much to the chagrin of the ruling menfolk. It even had royal approval, as the *Lady Cycling; What to Wear & How to Ride* guide published in 1897, pointed out: 'Her Majesty the Queen ... grasped the possibilities for good in the then new idea, and by her prompt action in ordering a couple of machines in the earliest days, she hall-marked the movement, and to her the thanks of all cyclists are due.'

Despite cartoons depicting catfights between bicycle-riding new women, as *Susan B. Anthony*, an American social reformer said in 1896: '[Bicycling] has done more to emancipate women than anything else in the world. I stand and rejoice every time I see a woman ride by on a wheel.'

It was effectively the first mode of transport that women had ever ridden entirely alone, and that gave them untold personal freedom. What's more, it facilitated romance for both sexes. As the *Lady Cycling* guide put it rather euphemistically: 'People go out to dinner – on bicycles. They pay surprise visits by moonlight – on bicycles . . .'

Similarly, the 1897 etiquette guide *Manners for Men* acknowledges that 'The seaside season is prolific in these chance acquaintanceships – "flirtations" as they perhaps be called. Bicycling is well known to favour them . . .'

The advice, of course, was to shun any sexual opportunity presented on two wheels: 'Should any young man become acquainted with a girl in this manner, let him show his innate chivalry by treating her in every way as he would wish his own sister to be treated in similar circumstances.' He was, however, encouraged to 'help ladies as much as possible by pushing their machines up the hills for them'.

But what people did and what they ought to do have always been quite different things, and photographs from the era prove that bicycling together at the seaside was one of the simpler romantic pleasures of the Victorian era.

Still, it was photography that was the real romantic game changer. In the 1860s, the fashion for creating photo albums out of 'carte de visites' – thin portrait prints – took hold. Exchanging photos was a kind of flirtation, but you could even buy photographs of celebrities and royalty. Well-to-do Victorian women would paste these in albums in amongst the friends and family pictures and relish the ambiguity of presenting an album that suggested their social connections and encounters could extend to the great and the good, the rich and famous.

And of course, there were erotic photos – the demand for which reached its peak in the 1880s, a demand supplied by French photographic studios which sold them under the counter and smuggled them in the post to England where they were surreptitiously distributed by the first porn dealers. While it's entirely likely daring couples might have viewed these images of models together, exchanging naked selfies would remain decades away.

Still, tamer romantic images were popular in Victorian parlours, and they were produced by stereographs – two images viewed together through a stereoscope to create a single three-dimensional picture. What were the favourite subjects? You've guessed it – love and relationships.

In 1888, the first personal camera, the Kodak, was launched. Now, people could take pictures of themselves without having to visit a proper photographic studio, and in Victorian Lonely Hearts ads, which were experiencing a revival at the end of the nineteenth century, the line 'photos exchanged' began to appear.

And it was just in time for a boom-time in personals – between 1870 and 1900, there were twenty publications dedicated to Lonely Hearts ads on the news-stands. Placing an ad in the *Matrimonial News* cost sixpence for forty words and ads were now starting to adopt a recognisable format; age, occupation, wealth – even details of any personal financial difficulty, which compared with today's dating ads seems surprisingly upfront. Advertising for a wife to move abroad with them, most commonly India and North America, was also common. The 1880s saw increased ads from working-class men and women. Take this ad from 1884:

William, a gas fitter, having been employed by one firm for over 10 years intends resigning and commencing business for himself; is desirous of corresponding with a lady about his own age – namely 33 – with a little means preferred. Advertiser is of a very kind and cheerful nature, and would make a good and attentive husband. Editor has address.

Suddenly people from all walks of life were prepared to invest in their romantic futures.

But they were also more open to being exploited, as a host of prosecutions for fraud reaching court at the end of the nineteenth century revealed. There were also a number of women who ended up single mothers as a result of dalliances with men they thought they would marry, met through ads.

As well as personal ads, some of these publications were now also running marriage agencies. But while the automatic discretion of the Lonely Hearts ad made them relatively unthreatening to use, they had to work hard to inspire confidence in their clients: 'With a view to ensuring strict secrecy in the matter of interviews, the Management have furnished the editor with commodious private premises in the vicinity of the publishing office, where such complete arrangements have been made for the convenience of visitors that they may call without fear of meeting with one another.'

A special notice printed in an October 1884 edition of the *Matrimonial Gazette* even went on to compare the struggles of the matrimonial agency to that facing technology: 'Steam, the greatest invention of the age, met with the most determined and inveterate opposition from all classes of the public, and it was only by the obstinate persistency of the constructor of the *Rocket* that our present lightning mode of transit became an accomplished fact.'

Rocket is a bit of an overreaching euphemism when you think about it, but needless to say there were some people who weren't permitted any of these opportunities, and that was the LGBT community. In fact, 'community' would be entirely anachronistic, given what queer individuals were up against at this time, 'secret society' would be more apt.

In 1861, the Offences Against the Person Act formally removed the death penalty for buggery. But by 1885, the Criminal Law Amendment Act had come into force instead. Making private homosexual acts, as well as any kind of street crawling or public proposition illegal, its charge of 'gross indecency' did not actually stipulate what exactly such acts might be. As for the now legendary image we have of Queen Victoria holding her lace-mittened hands to her ears, refusing to accept the existence of lesbians, it probably is a myth. Instead, it's thought that the law writers did not try to explain to her what lesbians might get up to in the privacy of their own bedrooms because they did not know how to explain it.

It was under the Criminal Law Amendment Act that Oscar Wilde found himself tried for gross indecency and imprisoned for two years, despite being technically married to a woman. Known as 'sexual inverts', homosexuals had, after all, been identified as a separate species to heterosexuals by scientists of the period.

Still gay men and women did meet and tarry, if not marry. There are the diaries of Anne Lister of Shibden Hall, West Yorkshire, to give us details on just how difficult it was to conduct life as a lesbian, even if one was born privileged and of independent financial means, as Anne was. Known as 'Gentleman Jack' to Yorkshire locals, Lister used a secret code to protect her correspondence with her lover Eliza Raine, and diary entries detailing her affairs over the years.

Take this from 1818: 'At 11 ¾ set off to Halifax . . . looking about me in every direction for Miss Browne . . . I think I succeeded in making myself agreeable . . . Paid her beauty several compliments and told her she was the best-dressed girl in town or neighbourhood.'

Or this about a later lover whom she was no longer so infatuated with: 'A little after 6, awakened by a rap at my door. It was M—, who had arrived by the mail . . . I certainly did not seem in extasies [sic] at seeing her but pretended I was half-asleep. She thought she should have found me at my studies. Did not take much persuading to get into bed and gave me one kiss immediately.'

In the 1850s, London was the scene of secret 'drag balls' and alternative guides to night life would tell you what saloons, coffee houses or streets to frequent if you wanted to be picked up. Outside of the capital it was much more difficult. After 1885, stories of prosecutions under the Criminal Law Amendment Act frequently made the press although they concentrated on cases in the capital city despite there being ample prosecutions around the country. Meanwhile, well-to-do men seeking homosexual adventures, including the author Somerset Maugham and Lord Alfred Douglas, followed the example set by Lord Byron some fifty years earlier and embarked on a kind of Mediterranean sex tourism to get their needs met; Greece, Turkey and Italy, in particular Naples, Sicily and the island of Capri became their sexual Eden.

But in the late Victorian era, England was not the only place where the British, whatever their sexual orientation, sought love. Colonialism meant thousands of Brits were living in India, Rhodesia and Ceylon, to name but a few locales – and they were as keen to hear 'I love you' from their native neighbours as they were one another.

Sir George Goldie, the creator of Nigeria, left Britain in 1877 for West Africa, where he spent three years living with an Arab girl in Egyptian Sudan. James Brooke, the white raja of Sarawak enjoyed a love affair with a Sarawak prince. Somehow relationships in the colonies helped them escape the oppressive late-Victorian contempt for sexual pleasure – abstinence was actually believed to be unhealthy in a hot climate.

For those who came to the colonies married and left their families behind, native companions kept them sane (suicide by drinking or shooting was not uncommon). Earlier in the eighteenth century, white plantation owners in the West Indies had frequently formed liaisons with black women – Samuel Taylor, the richest early Victorian planter in Jamaica, owned several estates, with a family on each. In India, Anglo-Indian women were held up as a beauty ideal, and every grade of relationship from mistress-hood to marriage socially acceptable. And in Southern Africa, there was a culture of *'nkotshane'* – 'boy wives' – by which Imperialist miners employed local boys to keep house and service them sexually, even expecting them to dress in drag and forbidding them from ejaculating. From Macao to Malaya, white men formed relationships with native men and women, sometimes short-lived and purely sexual, sometimes taboo-crushingly romantic. Then, in 1909, *The Crewe Circular* put an end to cross-colonial relationships by warning new recruits of the 'disgrace and official ruin which will certainly follow', should they enter into relationships with native women. It was official – enter a mixed-race relationship, however casual, at your peril.

The final decades of the Victorian era, known as the *'fin de siècle'*, was a time of artistic freedom, social shift, and a lot of discussion about sexual pleasure. Men's and women's roles were being redefined while the scientist Havelock Ellis asserted that women's sexual experiences should be as enjoyable for them as they were for men. Those of a kinky persuasion could find likeminded playmates in fashion magazines, where they had cleverly infiltrated the advice columns with a discussion of tight lacing and other kinds of restriction under the pretext of a debate on style and fit. Meanwhile, illustrated weekly magazines such as *London Life* and *Fun* hosted fetish-based correspondence. But Victorian literature liked to suggest otherwise with characters such as Jane Eyre rewarded for her modesty and plainness, while Madame Bovary or Sue Bridehead of *Jude the Obscure* reached their comeuppance for indulging their baser instincts. Meanwhile, themes of vampirism, degeneration, hysteria and syphilis were also taking their hold on the popular imagination, presented as they were through the fiction of the day. Industrialisation had changed daily life beyond compare, and sexuality had become the focal point for every fear about how modern life was evolving.

But not everybody was so reactionary. In 1897, a magazine called *The Adult* was founded by the Legitimation League which campaigned for changes to the bastardy, divorce and marriage laws. *The Adult* encouraged people to meet outside of their social class via the Lonely Hearts ads it carried. It sounds obvious to us, but focusing on personality compatibility rather than similar social standing was the purpose, and, radically, it encouraged relationships across class boundaries. A year later, on the other side, campaigner and journalist W. T. Stead sought to do the very opposite. After successfully campaigning for the age of consent to be increased from thirteen to sixteen in 1885 (it had been raised from twelve to thirteen a decade before with the Offences Against The Person Act), in 1898 he founded the Wedding Ring, a marital agency with the decorum-conscious middle classes in mind. It worked by holding two collections – one containing photos of its clients, the other information on their thoughts, beliefs, hobbies and interests. Clients were invited to browse both at its central London offices and introductions could then be made. It also issued a monthly magazine called the *Roundabout* which functioned to connect members.

Finally, the marriage agency was acceptable, even if women – the 'New Women' – opting to shun marriage altogether were not. But it was those ideas about social class that were to percolate into the Edwardian era, slowly beginning to change the social make-up of Britain one aristocrat at a time . . .

Chapter Four

The Edwardians: Buccaneer
boss-brides; maids on the make

If Victorian dating was characterised by romance, Edwardian love was characterised by revelry. While Queen Victoria had been deep in mourning for her beloved Albert, her son, Bertie, a.k.a. the Playboy Prince, had established a party scene unlike any in Europe. As Prince of Wales, he was forced to take the stand in a divorce trial as a witness to the impropriety of one Lady Mordaunt, defending his visits and communications with her as innocently platonic, even though he was already married to Princess Alexandra at the time. When he became king, his alleged indiscretions did not stop, it just became easier to manage the gossip.

To be part of Bertie's social scene was to be at the epicentre of the most bombastic clique. And there was a whole wealth of women who wanted to party with him – not only the Parisian demi-mondaines – lavishly jewelled and dressed noblewomen, many already married to Paris' Great and Good, who were looking for a little adventure – but namely the Buccaneer brides, who ventured over from America to husband-hunt amongst the English elite. In the past, Old New Yorkers had visited London without any intention of casting the net, mainly due to the fact that the

English had supported the South during the Civil War. Anglophobia amongst East Coasters was rife and this manifested itself as a kind of snobbishness. But when these spirited young American heiresses realised that London society was easier to crack than that of haughty New York, they reset their courtship compasses, flooding London in their hundreds. Lady Cora in *Downton Abbey* was one of a thousand opportunistic others.

It may sound like a phrase redolent of Beyoncé feminism, but 'self-made girls' was the expression of the day. These women went to singing and drawing and dancing lessons, they read and studied poetry, science, geography and languages. They were on the make in that way unique to Americans, and the Prince of Wales loved them. Not only were American girls the best dressed, but they had strong, lean bodies and good teeth, even before the advent of boot-camp workouts and Invisalign braces. Soon the high-profile couturier Charles Worth announced he would only dress American girls, for they had what he most admired: 'figures, francs and faith'.

They also had an ability to flirt and laugh and interact socially which was quite at odds with their English female counterparts. Oscar Wilde appreciated the American girl for 'her extraordinary vivacity, her electrical quickness of repartee, her inexhaustible store of cautious catchwords'. Americans talked more, and more easily, and young American couples were frequently left unchaperoned which made the females infinitely less stilted in male company.

Of course, once the Prince partied with the Buccaneers, so did everybody else. A Buccaneer bride became desirable, particularly if you were an English aristocrat with empty coffers. English gentlemen did not work, whether they were wealthy or not. And if the American heiresses had heard the expression, 'you can't buy class', they were hair-rollering right over it. Soon English gentlemen with scant means were spending the last of what they had on trips to the States with the sole purpose of ensnaring an heiress. San Francisco was a good spot, as well as Newport, New Hampshire and, of course, New York. However, even New York women were beginning to lose their appeal; they were too talkative, too forthright, and required no courting. They also had hordes of other competing admirers. Instead, the English aristocracy swiftly moved on to beauties from the Mid-West. So populous and fruitful did these marriages prove to be that many diplomats regarded them as good for Anglo-American relationships full stop. But as America recovered from the Civil War, and began to establish itself on the world stage, so the Bucanneers began to look further afield, and an English husband no longer carried the same cache. By the time Edward died in 1910, so the rambunctious London court scene that had attracted so many transatlantic lovelies died with him. The era of the Buccaneer bride was laid to rest with the King.

Despite the glamour popularised by the Buccaneer brides, and authors such as Mrs Pritchard, famous for her book *The Cult of Chiffon*, in which she praised more delicate lingerie and 'frou-frouing' draperies, dressing was never to be at the expense of tastefulness, and contemporary etiquette books carefully set out their rules for conveying decorum through one's dress. After all, up until 1914, if a girl of seventeen went to the opera in Paris or London with her hair down, she and her chaperones (distinguished by their dark day dresses) were sent to one of the higher balconies.

As Mrs Pritchard advised, firstly, 'Don't whatever the fashion may be, wear a lot of jewellery.' Secondly, 'Don't wear a number of diamonds or other precious stones by day; it is never in good taste.' Thirdly, 'Don't wear a large number of rings; it looks vulgar, and does not show the beauty of the rings or of the hands.' And fourthly, 'Don't wear a fine gown and shabby boots: to do so stamps a woman at once.'

The key silhouette for women of the Edwardian era was achieved mainly by virtue of the 's-shape' corset, tightly laced at the waist to force the hips back, thereby thrusting the bosom forward in what was known as a 'pointer pigeon' shape.

Combined with the right petticoats, skirts and bodice, this was covered with either a full gown, or an elaborate blouse and full gored skirt, often with a 'leg of mutton' sleeve which was meant to contrast with a tiny, trained and belted waist. The only difference between daywear and evening wear, as with Victorian fashion, was a much lower cut neckline of the bodice, which could be concealed with an elaborate necklace if company called for it. Hair dyeing was a no-no, and only a little make-up was allowed, with cakey foundation absolutely discouraged, mainly because it forced women to keep a Botox-tight smile in order not to crack it. As Mrs Pritchard had it again, 'The paste clings to the skin in such a manner that for the desired countenance to be achieved, emotions, whether they be joy or sorrow must be supressed.' Overall, young women were encouraged to look youthful without excessive adornment or false aid. Natural beauty was what would attract a man.

The American designer Charles Dana Gibson began to draw illustrations of what came to be known as 'the Gibson Girl', depicting the woman of the age in all her finery, capturing the outfits worn for leisure including horse-riding and golf. However, what was stylish was also threatening – the sporty, easier-of-movement ensemble of the Gibson Girl was also adopted as daywear by the New Woman, and so still receiving heavy criticism for the message it conveyed about a lady's moral fibres. As one female writer of the era observed, 'they do well to keep to their own clothes. An air of masculinity, however slight, goes against the woman who would be successful in the eye of the public and on platforms. Her frills and her laces are, in the meantime, a weapon.'

As Mrs Pritchard made even more explicit, 'Can one wonder that marriage is so often a failure, and that the English husband of such a class of woman goes where he can admire the petticoat of aspirations?'

The exaggerated and stylised body shape of the Gibson Girl was also controversial. With a large bottom and enhanced bosom to match, she resembled a fully clothed, proto-Page Three girl, and was modelled on Gibson's wife, of whom he said, 'if you have a canary you must let it sing'. But some men hated her, including commentator Dion Clayton Calthrop, who pronounced Gibson Girl-alikes 'awful' and remarked, 'They seemed to have lost their heads, their bodies, and their sense of proportion in colour . . . They looked like crazy housemaids.'

For men, meanwhile, 'moderation in all things', rather than 'the craze for the decidedly "different" ' was to be the motto, as set out in an article from the *Ladies' Home Journal* of 1907, written by one Frederick Taylor Frazer. Whether dressed for business or leisure, the elegant Edwardian gentleman wore a modestly coloured three-piece suit, with a white shirt, simple necktie, and bold colouring only allowed in a cravat, where worn. Handkerchiefs were white with a coloured border only, where colour was enlisted at all. Trouser turn-ups and up-brimming hats were frowned upon, and collars on shirts were to be cut modestly high – 'high enough to conceal the anatomical protuberance in front'. As for the evening jacket or tuxedo, 'it is not permissible at any gathering attended by women except the quiet dinner at home ... it is not in good form at a ball, a reception, the opera, a formal call or a celebration in which women participate'. Men accessorised with plain boots, gloves and walking sticks. Moustaches, meanwhile, were neat and waxed.

Interestingly, androgyny secretly flourished amongst Edwardian men. Take this letter from an anonymous gentleman to the *Daily Mail* in 1906:

> Tight-lacing is not only useful in producing the tiny waist so much admired by the male sex, but it is a delightful sensation. I commenced to wear corsets about twenty years ago, when as a lad I took part in private theatricals dressed as a girl, and I had to be very considerably tightened in to produce the necessary figure. I was so delighted with the feeling of wearing them that I have stuck to corsets ever since. I was first attracted to my wife by her small waist, and although she is now the mother of two little girls, she still retains her dainty figure.

Similarly, *The Queen* newspaper advised on the male wearing of earrings thus: 'If you do not think you will look ridiculous, only conspicuous, and do not mind, that is well.'

If dress afforded more scope for sensual expression, manners around courtship continued to evolve in favour of women's increasing emancipation. In 1891, a case had reached court concerning whether a wife must live with her husband. It was decided that she had the right to free movement and he could not use force to keep her with him – another small but pioneering victory in the quest for female liberty.

Women's magazines, much like today, often featured male writers offering their view on women. In an article for the American publication *Ladies' Home Journal* in 1907, a self-confessed 'Bachelor' wrote quite radically, 'I have often agreed with William Morris that ... men were naturally meant to be cooks and housemaids, and performed those duties far better than women. I go further and agree ... to the belief that women and not men ought to be priests and doctors, and that their work lies there.' Granted, this did not really explain why he had persisted in his bachelordom, but it does demonstrate that some men were prepared to make it known that they held women in high intellectual esteem.

However, women were still not to be overeducated lest they became bores – a little French and dancing was thought adequate for the middle to upper Classes, and just because womankind was now acknowledged capable of intellectual strivings didn't mean she was to be treated with any less gentility. Etiquette manuals were still inter-mittently consulted, and provided a wealth of information on social propriety.

Men, in particular, faced explicit instruction on just what kind of man they should be. In the 1902 handbook *Etiquette for Men*, for example, the ideal man was described as 'the well-bred, well-dressed, well-groomed gentleman; a man who is chivalrous, brave, strong, yet gentle, not painfully perfect, yet with complete control of his temper and his language, and who possesses a strong sense of honour and abundant humour'. Basically, David Beckham with a better command of English. But even Becks might not stand the book's test of well dressed, given that 'The man who looks really well in a dress suit is he who gets into it every night of his life.' Perhaps the authors were really imagining a proto-James Bond.

And then there was the matter of chivalry, newly shaken by the social change beginning to happen to women ('It is a moot point whether it is a more difficult matter for a man or for a woman'). Take, for example, offering to help a lady with a tower of parcels – 'Things have arrived at such a state that a lady, though perhaps unwillingly, would be suspicious of any man who would make such an offer, and the man would have exactly the same thought of the woman who would accept it.' Still, the bottom line was resolute: 'Never allow it for a moment to be seen that you were not expecting to have to salute her.'

If a social interaction reached the stage of a repeat face-to-face meet, calling cards and the distribution of them was still riddled with protocol. Cards were to be white, ivory or cream with no other decoration or border, and the gender of the card owner should not be discernible from its style. Copper plate was considered the most elegant font, and only the name and address should be listed. Married ladies left three cards upon calling at a friend's, two of which were her husband's, while unmarried ladies were not to leave cards for men on any occasion. And then there were new rules about the telephone, by which an invitation to an event should never be given 'for fear of engaging a person where they do not wish to be engaged'.

The process of calling, meanwhile, was particularly fraught for gentlemen – 'there are perhaps few things in life a man dreads more', reasoned *Etiquette for Men*, even claiming that a man often married in order 'to relieve him of these duties'.

Luckily, *Good Form* by Lucie Heaton Armstrong was one book to come to a befuddled gent's rescue.

On a date, it notes, 'A gentleman precedes a lady in entering a theatre, in order to make way for her. He gets her programme, offers her refreshments, helps her on with her cloak, and looks after her comfort in every possible way.'

And yet, 'He should pay her every attention in his power, but never in such a way as to make her the subject of remark.'

For a lady, perfecting a gentile laugh was actively encouraged, especially after a story circulated about a light opera star called Florence St John who had actually rehearsed hers for a scene in a production called *Madame Favart* and set the benchmark thereafter. Flashing teeth when smiling, however, was heavily frowned upon.

Dinners and day dates continued, as they had done in the Victorian era, only 'play-acting' or any of the kind of charades and dressing up that had previously been deemed as relatively innocent entertainment was now regarded as unseemly. As for masquerade balls, which offered 'a false opportunity for indecorous behaviour for men and women alike', upstanding Edwardians were reminded that 'the mask is a flimsy disguise at best' and so better to act as if they weren't wearing one at all.

For the lower classes, the music hall remained a prime place for a date, and with more shows aimed at women – the script of *A Gaiety Girl* featured actresses that married into the nobility, for example – it started to transform the venue as a place good girls were allowed to venture. Meanwhile, ragtime was all the musical rage, and with ragtime came dancing. Direct from America came the cakewalk, the bunny hug, the turkey trot, the grizzly bear, the crab step, the kangaroo dip, the horse trot and the Boston. Next followed South American dances – the Brazilian maxixe and the tango. When the gramophone was invented in 1877, dancing at home – or at least practising at home ahead of a public dance – only increased the night fever. Slightly less elegant a dating venue but nonetheless a popular one was the Sunday afternoon bandstand where courting couples could carouse to the strains of a colliery band.

For upper class couples, the London 'season' was still very much a part of Edwardian dating life. Debutantes fought for Queen Alexandra's favour, mainly because, as a contemporary etiquette manual put it, 'the debutante whose appearance evokes a pleased comment from Her Majesty is always safe to be one of the beauties of her season'.

At a dance or ball, men were encouraged to make the first move in securing not just one but a whole evening's dance partners, and then to ensure the dance actually happened by first asking 'May I have the pleasure of a dance with you,' or 'Will you give me the next dance?' before writing his initials on her programme and hers on his. Partners were not allowed to dance multiple times with one another unless engaged 'for it makes her an object of remark, which is always embarrassing and sometimes painful' and keeping a partner waiting was seen as the heart of rudeness. Despite the exacting etiquette, there were plentiful opportunities to subtly insinuate special affections. From fetching a lady an ice, to escorting her to her carriage at the end of the evening and ensuring she was suitably draped in her furs, the protocol of the ball left ample opportunities for impressing a beautiful partner, usually beginning and ending with the depth and sincerity of your bow.

But it was 'tea time' that provided both available and already married well-to-do men and women of the age with an opportunity for sexual frisson. Husbands, in particular, were actually expected to go out to tea, even with other men's wives, if not out to their club, and it was not rare for them to find themselves to be the only caller once they arrived at a lady's invitation. Servants knew to stay clear and an invitation to 'tea' was soon widely accepted as a euphemism for more, the equivalent of today's 'coming up for coffee'. Meanwhile, at country weekends away, hostesses in the know would often arrange married guests' bedrooms so as to make it all the easier for them to 'access' one another once everybody – including their actual spouses – were safely asleep.

Still, protecting reputations was vital. If you flaunted your affair you could find yourself at risk of being 'cut', an Edwardian term for being socially ostracised. What's more, the general consensus remained that indulging sexuality was bad for society at large. Published in 1908, the most influential book on the topic, *The Sexual Question*, written by an Austrian psychiatrist called August Forel, asserted, 'Photography and all the perfected methods of reproduction of pictures, the increasing means of travel which facilitate clandestine sexual relations, the industrial art which ornaments our apartments, the increasing luxury and comfort of dwellings, beds etc., are at the present day, so many factors in the science of erotic voluptuousness.'

If you were working class and in service, the strictures were even more severe.

In the Edwardian era, nearly 40 per cent of working-class women were employed in domestic service. Servants working in large houses were under a strict obligation not to engage 'followers'. Although this could mean family and friends, it really referred to romantic partners, or potential ones, and any servant found fraternising with another in the same house faced punishment. Depending on the severity of the misdemeanour, this could result in anything from a 'tongue-lashing' to having one's paltry afternoon off retracted, to, in the worst case, dismissal without references. For many young girls let go without references, their only option thereafter was prostitution.

Still, servants did form relationships with one another, although there was even a hierarchy within flirting. Housemaids favoured footmen while kitchen maids tended towards outdoor staff, and in the event they wanted to be together, the custom was to resign from service together. However, as long as the relationship had been conducted discreetly, and the correct protocol was followed when announcing it to the master and mistress of the house, they might even occasionally help with your sending off. When Jean Hibbert who worked in service for the Duchess of Richmond of Goodwood Hall announced that she had fallen in love with the head gardener, the Duchess actually offered to pay for the wedding and allowed the kitchen staff to make a sumptuous feast and three-tiered cake.

Scullery maids, meanwhile, all too often found themselves at the bottom of the social pile – and often recipients of the master of the house's (or his son's) attentions. As in the Victorian era, should a master choose to exercise his '*droit de seigneur'*, as it was known, over a maid, she could hardly refuse him. Should she find herself pregnant, it was all too easy for him to insinuate she'd been inappropriately involved with either another member of staff, or, if he wanted to minimise gossip amongst the rest of the staff about who, a visiting courier or the like was a better alibi. Dismissal was instant and the future prospects of a pregnant former maid with no references? About as good as those of single pregnant women in the developing world today.

Life and love was of course easier if you were out of service, where holidays became crucial opportunities for a little romantic relief. But even holidays came with risks. A *Woman's Weekly* from 1914 carried this cautious advice for 'Making Friends on Holiday': 'Don't play with Cupid, little girl, by the sea . . . Those darts of his may make but pinpricks but even pin-pricks can hurt, and they leave scars.'

The caution against a little holiday nookie was, as ever, hinged on the loss of female reputation, and the article wrapped up by ominously warning: '. . . the newly formed seaside acquaintance can only form his opinion of you from the way you behave while in his company.'

However, being a mistress was still an option for an attractive young woman on the make, provided he didn't abandon you and leave you with an illegitimate child in the process. For women to take lovers was quite socially unacceptable – and yet aristocratic ones did on an occasional basis. To some extent this inequality was influenced by the example of the very beautiful Queen Alexandra, who, despite her looks and husband's frequent infidelities, is not said to have ever embarked upon her own.

Engagements were still heavily socially codified, as this advice from *Etiquette for Women: a book of modern modes and manner*, published in 1902, goes to show: '[. . .] if you are a very wealthy young lady, or of somewhat higher social position, a man is in duty bound to ask your parents' and guardian's permission to pay your attention, or to win you if he can'. Meanwhile, 1902's *Etiquette for Men* advised males not to show they were in love: 'etiquette demands that a man shall at least appear as his ordinary self, and not make the fact patent to the most casual observer'. So much for the unadulterated joy of an unfolding love match.

To make a proposal, a man, no matter how shy, was advised to go to the lady direct, rather than to write to her, thus ushering the real tradition of proposing as we understand it today. And if she didn't accept immediately? 'You must fall in with her wishes without protest; at least without too much protest.'

And yet there was a sense that the tradition was becoming tedious for all involved. 'The interview is a business interview, embarrassing to both men perhaps, but it has to be gone through, for on it much of the happiness of the young couple depends.'

Expectations of women's purity were beginning ever so gently to shift too. A story published in a 1907 edition of the *Ladies' Home Journal*, entitled, 'The Confessions of an Engaged Couple', whereby the pair admit previous romances to one another, delicately demonstrates how women were now allowed to admit to having been in love before becoming betrothed.

When it came to engagement rings, they were to be given as soon as the betrothal was 'a settled matter'. What's more, 'the ring itself should be a handsome, serviceable one, not too fanciful in design'. It was important that a woman didn't have to take it off every time she wanted to wash her hands, for example. It was also during this period that the ring came to be placed on the third finger of the left hand, where it remained until it was replaced by the wedding ring.

Once engaged, couples were not to flaunt the fact. 'Do not spoil a party by a complete and selfish absorption in each other, and at a dance do not dance together constantly.' Discretion, noted the contemporary etiquette guides, was the real charm: 'What a girl likes most in a man is a never failing, quiet attention to, and care for her tastes, needs, wishes.'

And if it just so happened that her parents insisted on her chaperonage during your engagement, you had to suck it up. 'You can only take it as the leaven in the lump in your happiness,' advised *Etiquette for Men*.

In the event of breaking off an engagement, 'it is kinder and less painful to the lady if it be allowed to be thought that the act is hers,' advised the etiquette of the day, and after letters, photographs, presents, and the engagement ring were returned, it was the duty of the mother of the lady to announce the unfortunate news.

There was, however, a group of women who were refusing all such attentions. The New Woman had demands for education, economic independence and sexual equality – including the vote. She smoked, she drove, she wore practical clothing. She upset every expectation about femininity. And she usurped expectations where marriage and children were concerned. As a popular essay of the age entitled 'Woman Adventurers' put it, 'Shall women propose? Well, if they can stand the risk of being accepted, surely yes.'

Still, not all men were dissuaded. One contemporary source complained:

The least that Man can do to stamp out these shameless rebels is to show his personal disgust of them as individuals. He is doing nothing of the kind. Instead, he is positively frequenting their society. He lunches, teas, and dines with them at their unfeminine and independent institutions – clubs – showing his preference, indeed, with astonishing emphasis, for these abandoned haunts to that of the rigid drawing room which his 'ideal' inhabits. And the galling part of the whole thing is that these brazen young women are deliberately and openly disavowing all man's conceptions and wishes of what they ought to be doing and thinking.

It might have been fashionable to pour scorn on New Women but they invited the attentions of a certain kind of male. In particular, they sought out – and initiated – information about sex. While reliable mainstream medical information was only addressed formally to 'married' women, it was almost certainly reaching the hands of dating-age women who wanted to protect themselves against unwanted pregnancy and STIs.

The fact is, Edwardian men and women were having premarital sex and using contraception to help them conceal the fact. Rubber condoms were first available around the 1870s. They weren't disposable; instead you washed them with carbolic soap. Then soluble pessaries started to be sold in the 1880s. By 1908, the Lambeth Conference of Bishops noted 'with alarm the growing practice of the artificial restriction of the family', both inside and outside of marriage.

But good advice on contraception was harder to come by. *The Wife's Handbook*, by Dr Henry Arthur Allbutt, first published in 1886, ran into fifty-six editions, and had a whole section dedicated to 'avoiding conception', offering advice on the fertility cycle (incorrect advice, it must be said); the withdrawal method, and a variety of home-made contraceptives such as a sponge doused in quinine, pessaries, and even 'letters' – otherwise known as condoms. It also offered some rather radical views on how a woman could ensure her life partner was venereal-disease free: 'Before giving her consent to marry [. . .] She should also be sure that he is free from any contagious disease which can be communicated through sexual relations. [. . .] I should like to see it the custom for women or their parents to demand a recent medical certificate of freedom from syphilis from all men proposing marriage. In this matter false delicacy should be dropped.'

All this pragmatic advice might have sounded on the edge of revolutionary.

But it took another bevy of individuals to synthesise all these new and progressive ideas of love, sex, dating and the happy-ever-after: the Bohemians.

Influenced by the writings of Freud on the unconscious which sanctified acting on sexual impulse, and Charles Darwin's theory of mate competition which championed the ability of females to choose their partners, the Bohemians claimed to have deep feelings for their lovers – this was what gave them their moral validity in what they saw as a sea of fake marriages and economic arrangements.

Bigamy had been illegal since 1603 and homosexuality or 'gross indecency' newly outlawed in 1885, but Bohemians didn't care about the laws. Adultery might have been considered immoral but it definitely wasn't illegal if all parties were happy with the arrangement. The Bloomsbury

Group were described as 'a circle of people who lived in squares and loved in triangles'. But it was not only in Bloomsbury that artists were affecting these arrangements. In Hammersmith, the writer Robert Graves and his wife Nancy Nicholson lived in 'Free love corner' with an American, Laura Riding. They were joined by Geoffrey Phibbs, a poet and entomologist to create an awkward foursome that fell apart soon afterwards.

Then there was Christine Kühlenthal, wife of the painter John Nash, who brought to her marriage a girlfriend named Norah and lived in the Chiltern Hills, Gloucestershire. When Norah later married her boyfriend Charlie, Christine said, 'Charlie and I take it in turns to sleep with Norah, which again I think is very kind of him.'

In particular, the idea of the open marriage appealed strongly to the Bohemians. If they were to think radically about art, why not about relationships? In advocating open marriage, they were also rebelling against the prowess of the rich and titled who had long had alternative arrangements. It was left to the middle classes, meanwhile, to perpetuate the social orthodoxy of the nuclear family. Hence, dating for the Bohemians was effectively a life-long process; they did not 'settle' in any conventional sense of the word with their partners, married or otherwise. Instead, flirtations and seductions happened throughout their lifetimes.

Unlike the rest of society, the Bohemians held a much more relaxed attitude towards homosexuality. In 1908, the poet and activist Edward Carpenter published *The Intermediate Sex*, a cry to arms for homosexuality, which he saw as both superior to heterosexuality, and innate. At the same time, the Fitzrovian 'Psychological Society' doubled up as a pick-up joint for homosexual aesthetes. W. H. Auden, Lytton Strachey, painter Robert Medley, economist Maynard Keynes were all leading Bohemian homosexuals, 'out' to a subsection of society, despite the legal risks of being so.

But while the Bohemians were advocates of free and easy sexual engagement, the rest of the population was uneasy about the social shifts that were making hooking up more convenient but possibly less healthful. Ironically, the Suffragettes only added to this panic. Their slogan, 'Votes for Women' had a now-forgotten second part – 'Chastity for Men'. Adopted in response to the spread of venereal disease, their key belief was that men would benefit from aping the moral purity of women and they worried that easily available birth control without other rights such as access to education and the vote would leave women ever dependent on a secure legal marriage while men got to indulge their sexual proclivities. When a cure for syphilis was found by male scientists, Christabel Pankhurst went into denial, believing it a ruse to protect male sexual freedom: 'Always [men] want to sin and escape the consequences . . . they proclaim that they have found at last the cure for which they have been seeking through the centuries. A cure for sexual disease, which is of all diseases the most incurable.'

Instead, the Suffragettes presented a woman with two options: find a man who will consider you an equal and marry him sharpish, or opt for chaste spinsterhood. This was despite the fact that by 1913 more than 60 per cent of the Pankhurst organisation were married, as were all of its twenty-three organisers. Its core members, however, remained young, single women with Christabel, maintaining later that she had never married because she had never met a man who met her standards. A third option, to have a discreet same-sex relationship with a sister-in-arms, was never really vocalised, but rumoured to have been adopted by several notable members of the suffrage movement, including leading activist Flora Drummond, nicknamed 'The General' for her indomitable style when leading marches.

Soon Sir William Acton's belief that women's suffrage would quash men's sexual power was dismissed almost unilaterally as proof of the male supremacy they sought to temper. If men and women were to share more mutual pleasure in sex, love and marriage, it had to go.

This focus on the relationship between sexuality and public health also benefitted women in other ways. The female gynaecologist Elizabeth Blackwell used her scientific knowledge to assert some powerful new truths about female sexuality – firstly that removing healthy ovaries to cure everything from irregular periods to epilepsy had to stop. And, secondly, that 'the demands of women are greater than those of men, they desire more and more the thought and devotion of those they love'.

But just as concentrated enquiry into what made the girlfriends, wives and future mothers of England tick socially and sexually was on the horizon, war broke out across Europe. What women really wanted was going to have to wait.

Chapter Five

The First World War: Khaki fever and the Ladies in Black

If the outbreak of war meant civilian life would never again resemble what had gone before, *Vanity Fair* wouldn't initially let its readers know it. In 1914, before the shock of the deaths of 700,000 young men had been felt, the magazine was still trying to solve the riddles of contemporary relationships, guided by heavily gendered assumptions.

In 1914, Dorothy Dix wrote 'A man's love, no matter how ardent and passionate in the wooing days, soon settles down into a good, useful friendship and partnership sort of a feeling toward his wife, so that six months after marriage it's all one to him whether he married the Juliet of the balcony or Mary Jane of the kitchen.'

If the romantic scepticism wasn't enough, the notion of a kind of emotional eugenics, the responsibility for which was only carried by the fairer sex, also informed the writer's perspective: '. . . biologists tell us that a woman's love for her husband determines to a great extent the quality, mental and physical, of the children she bears'.

So the Victorian stereotype of the Angel in the House flittered and scrubbed her way right into wartime. And wartime propaganda was full of its own related feminine images. Women were depicted as passive and nurturing, tied to home and hearth and in need of protection. Men fought not only out of duty to their country, and a sense of personal honour, but to ensure the safety of their women-folk. And there were to be consequences if they betrayed them. Propaganda recruitment posters played on the idea that if a man was unfaithful to the country, it had serious consequences for your relationship: 'If your young man neglects his duty to his King and Country, the time may come when he will *Neglect You*.'

If women were at risk of being spurned, they could also be used to do the spurning. In August 1914, Admiral Charles Penrose Fitzgerald organised a group of thirty women in Folkestone to hand out white feathers, a symbol of cowardice, to young men not in uniform. The act was meant to shame 'slackers' into enlisting. The practice was soon adopted across the country and continued even beyond 1916 when conscription came into force.

One soldier and author, Compton Mackenzie, had a different interpretation, viewing the White Feather Movement as the action of 'idiotic young women who were using white feathers to get rid of boyfriends of whom they were tired'. Whether true or not, what is certain is that men began to loathe the women who were calling them and their friends out on their real or imagined cowardice. In the public imagination, their accosting reminded many of the way prostitutes went about soliciting clients.

But while one coterie of women was secretly vilified for scorning men, another was openly vilified for adoring them. By 1914, more men were dressed in army fatigues than civvy clothes, and the sheer number of these uniformed hunks was thought to induce a psychological condition called 'khaki fever' in Britain's women.

With the age of consent newly raised from thirteen to sixteen, the fact that these amorous hordes were young girls in particular – aged thirteen, fourteen and fifteen – alarmed the authorities and the general public. Even more alarming was the revelation that these army groupies spanned class boundaries, with as many well-heeled middle-class ladies falling for soldiers as working-class ones.

Challenging the convention that good girls were chaste ones, anxiety was situated around the 'amateur' – a girl who would put out without requiring payment – somehow even worse than a prostitute – and the situation became even more inflammatory when new tented cities full of fatigue-clad young men sprang up across the country, with women soon inviting the officers to tea and singing around the piano. 'Another evil even more insidious and more degrading than drink has to be guarded against and fought', so pronounced Millicent Garratt Fawcett, and there are plenty of first-hand accounts from the period illustrating just what was going on. As Edith Sellers, writing in 'Boy and Girl War-products: their reconstruction', observed, 'Some of them certainly behaved themselves very badly, simply pestering the younger of the soldiers by their "forthputfulness", lying in wait for them, seizing them by the arm as they passed ... I saw some English Tommies who were being pursued by girls, spring into an omnibus for safety.'

Curfews were placed on women in towns such as Grantham, prohibitions were placed on women's drinking; no opportunity to police women's sexual behaviour was wasted.

But in reality, 'khaki fever' was not so much about undue sexual attraction, as prohibited participation. Their chaperones may have vanished off to the frontline pretty much overnight, but at the beginning of the war, young women had no real role in the war effort, and they compensated for this by hanging out with those that were off to derring-do.

Once the majority of soldiers had cleared out to war, and women began to wear fatigues and take up all manner of patriotic duties themselves, the fever began to abate.

What women wore caused no similar outpouring of lust. If the masculine fashion of the New Woman had upset the Victorians and Edwardians, those living in the First World War had to accept that it was now not just a fact of daily life, but a matter of national security and patriotism that women were adorned, as unsexily as they may be, in knickerbockers and overalls. As Women's Land Army recruits advised, regardless of the trousers they now wore, they were 'English girls who expect chivalry and respect from everyone they meet'. Fabric was, ironically, not actually rationed during the First World War, but the need for increased movement meant skirts were now shorter and fuller, and loosely fitted blouses along with cardigan coats became de rigueur daywear. There was an unsuccessful attempt to bring in 'National Standard Dress', a one-shape-fits-all gown meant to serve as both day and evening wear, but while garments were skimpier, they were not necessarily sexier, with most women plumping for comfort over style.

But regardless of this arguably shabbier aesthetic, those in the factories and fields, and those in the trenches continued to cultivate their relationships. For if soldiers at the front had one another for companionship, it did nothing to assuage their stark need for correspondence with their loved ones back home. This was the golden age of the Great British postal service and up to twenty thousand bags of mail was sent to the French camps every day. The Defence of the Realm Act ensured that private correspondence from soldiers at the front was censored in order to ensure information of national security wasn't leaked, as evidenced by this extract from a letter from Lieutenant Erwin von Freiherr Pflanzer-Baltin to his fiancée Violet Murchison: '[. . .] don't be angry, my sweet darling, I shall never be able to tell you where I am or what I am doing, because that is classified and forbidden on pain of court-martial. I shall send you word of me as often as I can, but if you don't hear anything from me for a long time, you will know that I have been killed for the Fatherland'.

Still, contemporary letters reveal just how casual arrangements between the sexes could be and the kind of bravado with which young bucks had taken to the front line. Take this note sent from a twenty-year-old soldier called Geoffrey Boothby to the seventeen-year-old Edith Ainscow in July 1915:

Darling,

You now have a real live 'lonely soldier somewhere in France'. Only he's not very lonely. Also it's beastly conceited to imagine you hadn't got several others. Let us say 'another – er – boy in France' ... Knowing you as I do (having been in your company for, I believe, a period of four incomplete days all told), knowing you as I do, I repeat, I feel certain you will condone this temporary lapse from heartbrokenness under which I am supposed to stagger.

By the end of 1914, one year into the war, soldiers without a sweetheart to send them tunic buttons, Oxo cubes and suggestive photographs along with words of soothing and succour were advertising in papers and magazines for pen pals, friends, and potentially more. By 1915, British lonely soldier advertising was established in two publications – *The Link* and *T.P's Weekly* – and in some of the mainstream press. In one way, corresponding with a lonely soldier was seen as a patriotic duty. In France and Britain, correspondents were known as 'godmothers of war' and the recipients of their epistolary care, 'adopted sons', with the *Manchester Evening News* reporting that some ninety thousand were in correspondence by the end of the year. In Blighty, it worried the Home Office who considered the security risk of so many strangers exchanging letters with those on the front line. They envisioned Mata Hari-alikes enticing prime details of national security out of men desperate for a confidante and had some evidence that this was happening. So in May 1916 the government issued a notice to the press warning them from publishing letters and adverts, either for strangers to communicate with servicemen or for gifts or loans.

It was too late, for the exchange of many of these letters had already led to the so-called 'hasty marriage scare' in which women and men that had never physically met fixed up weddings after a relationship conducted purely by correspondence. On Christmas Day 1915, it led to the Bishop George Frodsham denouncing the practice in the *Cheltenham Chronicle*, warning that it led to 'a deplorable source of much unhappiness'. But it continued and in 1918 the *Liverpool Echo* ran the article, 'Should soldiers propose to girls they have not seen?'

Meanwhile, companionship adverts continued to appear in papers such as the *Daily Express* until the mid-1920s. Stipulating physical characteristics and photographs, and sometimes offering paid holidays, they also continued to be a foil for gay men and women seeking same-sex companionship.

The topsy-turvy conditions of wartime offered gay men and women as well as straight ample new opportunities to hook up. Soldiers on leave could meet other men in London's Piccadilly, attend all-male parties, or drink at venues such as the Golden Calf or the Criterion. But in the context of wartime, many men got it on with one another without ever considering it homosexual. Kissing in the face of front-line victory was frequently seen as a celebratory rather than an intimate act. Similarly, dressing up in drag made for popular troop entertainment and, after the war, military drag troops even toured the country.

Wartime romancers relished shore leave and the snatched weekend. But they were also blighted from the beginning by the most unsavoury of gooseberries: venereal disease. By December 1914, there were already 1230 cases of VD under British expeditionary force charge, with the rate seven times higher than that of Germany purely because the British government was in denial about it. Similarly, instructions that no men could return home until clean made for a huge amount of cases in French hospitals, some quarter of a million. By 1916, more than a hundred thousand soldiers had been admitted to hospitals in Britain. And then came the Defence of the Realm Act in 1918 which made it an offence for any woman suffering from VD to have intercourse with or invite intercourse with any member of His Majesty's forces. Women could even be detained for medical inspection.

Prostitutes were no longer thought the sole problem. The loose morals of wartime had 'infected' non-professional women's sense of propriety and many swarmed to training camps in towns such as Folkestone where they targeted in particular imperial troops from Canada and Australia, evidenced by the fact rates of VD rose to more than three times that of the British level.

It was even said that some women with VD offered to have unprotected sex with soldiers, the sole benefit of infection being that it would keep them from the front for a month or so longer while they recuperated.

Still, the war taught women about sex in other ways. Some fifty thousand young women, some even less than the minimum age of nineteen, flocked to join the Voluntary Aid Detachments. As the writer and nurse Vera Brittain explained, it fulfilled her sex education: 'I had never looked upon the male body of an adult male.' And yet, 'Short of going to bed with them, there was hardly an intimate service that I did not perform for one or another in the course of four years, and I still have reason to be thankful for the knowledge of masculine functioning which the care of them gave me.'

Although they had been growing in use since their invention in 1870, condoms during the First World War were scarce due to the Japanese takeover of Malaya which had resulted in a shortage of rubber. With teats for babies' bottles made a priority, ironically even more children were probably conceived as a result. Besides, the British government was at this point in denial about the extent of the problem and did not endorse condoms as a result.

Social purity thus became the order of the day. In a bid to clean things up, all sorts of activities were proclaimed undesirable and frivolous, including the theatre, music halls, cinema, nightclubs and tea shops. By 1914, there were 3500 cinemas in Britain, visited by half the population once a week. Pre-war cinemas even had women's patrols combing them for acts of indecency though the wartime labour shortage put an end to their inspection – not before they'd called time on the Rank Cinema in Finsbury Park, 'where couples were embracing each other all over the building, and were guilty of most unseemly behaviour'. Tea shops were another site of libidinous activity, culminating in 'The Tea Shop Scandal' where scantily clad waitresses served amorous customers, both couples and singles alike.

When the Prime Minister Lloyd George enforced early pub closing hours in 1915, nightclubs flourished. And young women were not about to relinquish their new-found freedom. In the autumn of 1915, a national newspaper published a story about the 'dining out girls', the new generation of single ladies who were taking the cities by storm by enjoying meals out on their meagre war-working wages without male companions. For once, the *Daily Mail* was actually quite celebratory of this display of female independence: 'most often they are in couples, though not infrequently one sees merry groups of three or four', and went on to herald their precocity as 'the beginning of the evolution of the business girl as a woman of the world'. But by January 1916, there were reports of widespread cocaine use among them, which the Defence of the Realm Act then outlawed by July of the same year.

Single men about town, meanwhile, were also beginning to be viewed less suspiciously. On an essay on bachelors published in a 1914 edition of *Vanity Fair*, writer Dorothy Dix observed: 'It is beyond denying, though, that the bachelor is looked upon askance, as one who has displayed almost super-natural foxiness in escaping trouble.' Yet coming to their defence, she explained, 'Many a man denies himself the love of a wife, and the feel of the arms of little children around his neck, and the joy of a home of his own, because he has had laid upon his shoulders the burden of an old mother's support', concluding that 'we can't do without them. They are a useful and beneficent institution – If only as material for the matchmaker and the tax-gatherer.'

Still, if living the single life was becoming gradually more acceptable and with wartime offering ample opportunity to play up, the scare of contracting VD and the risk of pregnancy remained the best contraceptive.

Amongst the middle and upper classes, accounts of the period tell us about weekend 'petting parties', 'where they [women] did not sleep with them [men], but cuddle, and the man would have an ejaculation, that sort of thing'.

Similarly, as one Lady Marguerite Tangye put it, 'If you were a bit attracted to someone you'd end up lying on the sofa with them when everyone had gone to bed. It just seemed a pleasant thing to do ...' It was judged more pleasant for the women than for the men. 'I remember sitting in a car fooling about with one man and he said, "I must get out and run round the block," cool himself off, I suppose. And some of them would go to the Bag of Nails, which was a sort of quite smart brothel-type place.'

For working-class men and women though, this kind of behaviour would not wash. At the heart of the Suffragettes' philosophy had been the notion that women had superior moral souls, and could police public behaviour more efficiently than men. This manifested itself anew in the establishment of two women's organisations, the Women's Police Service and the Voluntary Women's Patrols, to do just that.

In part a reaction to so-called khaki fever, the Women's Police Service was set up by Margaret Damer Dawson and

Mary Allen (both of whom had links to the militant suffra-gette Women's Social and Political Union) and had an interventionist intention, with members' mission being to warn both men and women about the dangerous ramifica-tions of immoral behaviour.

When Dawson and her assistants arrived in Grantham in 1915, they did so with the aim of cleaning up the town's behaviour. With a large military presence, the army general commanding the district gave them access to any building within a six-mile radius. This meant they could check if people were having illicit sex; what they found were hundreds of soldiers and women getting it on. This was serious stuff. Any soldier's wife found of drunkenness or prostitution could lose their army allowance, although the police did advise the WPS to cut them some slack on the basis that they had been 'deprived of the company and guidance of their husbands'. Any other woman was given a sanctimonious lecture. At about this time the term 'flap-per' first came into use – and it was not definitely not a compliment.

If that sounded draconian, the Voluntary Women's Patrols had even more puritanical clout. Wearing special armbands and always operating in pairs, by 1918 they had become a section of the Metropolitan Police, and by 1923 they would have full powers of arrest. Their job was to investigate sexual offences and to advise young girls on what kind of behaviour would protect them from running into trouble with lascivious men. Hired for their 'tact and experience', these thirty-, forty- and fifty-something women were paid six shillings plus expenses for an eight-hour working day which they spent in London, or in the vicinity of army camps and depots, patrolling in the dark with lanterns, on a mission to separate copulating couples, frequently on Sunday where people met on their day off after evening church services. London parks, including Norwood, Blackheath and Hyde Park were the site of much carnal mischief, and the chastised couples in Hyde Park soon started to spill onto Park Lane, which annoyed the police. No wonder they were nicknamed the 'interfering toads'.

But there was one group of men that the government and the interfering toads had not accounted for. In 1914, merchant seamen from countries across the Empire settled in port towns across the UK – London, Liverpool, Brighton, South Shields – to pay a crucial part in the war effort. Unable to reside outside of racially segregated boarding houses, they formed their own communities but had the chance to meet and mingle with working women who were no longer chaperoned and cossetted by their British menfolk. These Chinese, black and Asian sailors were an attractive proposition: well mannered, generous with money, fit, able and, most importantly, available where British men were absent.

Of course, they formed secret relationships with many of the women left behind, and even started families with them, many of whom they were forced to abandon when the authorities became aware of the couplings.

By the time the war ended, there were more than one million surplus women to every eligible man. But women had a new resourcefulness on their side. They could work, earn and save their own money, and were free of chaperones. Women were actually in a better position than ever before to choose their own mates.

Chapter Six

The Twenties: Hasty marriages
and petting parties

By the time the war was over, the relationship between the sexes had been forever changed and the dating game irrevocably altered. Young men came back from the front maimed, depressed and shell-shocked, if they came back at all. Married women had either to deal with these broken men or confront the fact they may be war widows, even before the age of twenty. A fear of communism, problems for the coal industry plus an economy depression, culminated in the General Strike of 1926. Life for most working men and women in post-war Britain was bleak.

But for those with land, money, property, or exceptional beauty, the torpor of wartime could be blasted away by partying. The Bright Young People, or Bright Young Things, as they have more commonly become known, were a group of artists, writers and socialites who had adopted a devil-may-care attitude to between-the-war living and cavorted with considerable glee as a result. Treasure hunts across London, car chases, country weekend orgies and all-night drinking formed the bedrock of their social activities, and their entanglements with one another rivalled that of the Bloomsbury set in their exuberance.

The Bright Young People were also effectively the first celebrities, featuring heavily in the new tabloid gossip columns of the day, utilising the power of branding to leverage sponsorship and promotions that only added to their notoriety.

When it came to looking the sybaritic part, fashion was crucial in giving the BYTs both a unique stylistic freedom and a bad name. Given their prime position in magazines, what they wore had an indelible impact on the style of the nation. Previously, the only women that had worn short hair had been prostitutes (if shaven as part of public humiliation) or nuns. Flappers occupied a space nowhere near between the two. Short hair, known as the bob or the shingle, was a grave affront to femininity and by the time the hairstyle had filtered down to the everyday girl on the street, it was a national threat to marriage: 'Shingles Leave Girls Single', ran one contemporary newspaper headline.

Clothes were deemed similarly indecorous. Surviving on a diet of single-spirit cocktails and cocaine, the Bright Young Things seemed to possess nothing but angles, perfect for wearing a style that sat best on the pin-thin. With this emphasis on a boyish figure, corsets, padding, bustles, and the generally hyper-feminine shaping of Edwardian dress was out. Instead, waists were dropped and hems lifted to calf height, allowing far more ease of movement for dancing and general racing about, although it wouldn't be until 1926 that hems rose above the knee. At the society wedding of the decade between the aristocratic Prince Albert, Duke of York and the commoner Lady Elizabeth Bowes-Lyon, Elizabeth shunned a more traditional gown and went for a heavily embroidered dress with a dropped waist. Day dresses sported pleated or tiered hems, evening dresses, fringing. Stockings morphed from dark wool and cotton to rayon in neutral tones. Everyday women dampened the shine by powdering their legs before a night out. Shoes were Cuban or hour-glass heeled with retaining straps suitable for all-night dancing.

Men, meanwhile, were enjoying a relaxation in style too, with sports clothes suddenly finding their way into everyday apparel (although only on the bodies of men with leisure time). Shorter jackets, 'Oxford bags' (a wider style of trouser), shirts with detachable collars, and, by evening, the tuxedo were part of a new male wardrobe which emphasised fit, flair, and range of movement.

Still, as ever, women carried a greater aesthetic burden. Any woman with sizeable breasts bandaged them to achieve the correct, sleek silhouette under a light, soft brassiere and a thin camisole. To her aid came something called the Symington Side Lacer, which fastened up under both arms, so flattening the breasts. As Barbara Cartland would describe them, the fashionable women of the day were 'enchanting, sexless, bosomless, hipless, thighless creatures'. For everyday women without access to class A drugs and who needed to eat to fuel their working lives, it was a tough time to be working such a demanding aesthetic.

Besides setting the fashion tone, the bright young things also inspired a unique lexicon, many of terms from which soon entered everyday English. While the term 'flapper' had originally referred to a young prostitute, it had evolved to mean a girl with a boyish figure just before the war. By the time it slipped into common parlance in England, it was one of multiple words that reveal just how valuable liberty and a shunning of social convention were to the inaugural flappers. 'Alarm clock' meant chaperone, and 'handcuff', engagement ring. Given this was the dawn of the motor age, car-related euphemisms also took hold, with 'oilcan' being used to refer to an imposter, and a dull person known as a 'flat tire'. The motorcar, meanwhile was a means to greater amorous adventure. Suddenly it was more convenient than ever to date someone who lived in a different town to you, although its primary benefit was the trips away from home altogether that it afforded, particularly to the seaside – and the ramifications that being off the local leash provided. As one man of the time put it, 'Asking a girl to Brighton meant sex', a slick and easy way to secure a seduction. Incidentally, the term 'plastered' for drunk also appeared around this time.

Meanwhile, for your average BYT, parties were big, bold extravaganzas. Dressing up to a theme was not uncommon, nor was dressing up as one another. Swimming pools and country homes were routinely commandeered as the venues du jour and eleven thousand nightclubs that existed in London by 1925 were very much their playground.

But not all of their escapades were the subject of envy. American actress Tallulah Bankhead, who once described herself 'as pure as the driven slush', was investigated by MI5, suspected of indulging in 'indecent and unnatural' acts with under-age boys at Eton College. She was also accused of lesbianism and of a generally debauched behaviour. Fortunately for her, Eton's then headmaster Dr C. A. Alignton refused to humour the claims and would not cooperate with the agents who came to interview him.

Then in 1922 came the case of Christabel and John Hugo Russell. Upon finding out that Christabel was pregnant, John claimed that she must have had an affair, given that they had never had full sexual intercourse. Christabel countered that their heavy petting could indeed have led to conception, yet three other men were named in court as her lovers and Christabel wrote to a friend, 'I have been so frightfully indiscreet all my life that he has enough evidence to divorce me about once a week.' After three trials, the House of Lords eventually declared the child legitimate. However wild life of the Bright Young Things burned on the surface, the rather more sombre instinct to uphold the status quo of marital bliss prevailed.

At the same time, the only ordinary people having anything like a similarly good time were the new generation of young women workers who flooded the cities and took up jobs as journalists, secretaries and shop girls. With their admittedly meagre yet still disposable incomes and their increasing freedom from watchful family and community eyes, they began to carve out new identities for themselves that were not tied to their mere status as an unmarried miss, wife or mother. They no longer needed chaperones. They no longer had to live under the auspices of their families. And, despite the depleted numbers of males, they were in a better position than ever to angle for the men they really wanted. And jazz, was the soundtrack to their seductions.

Jazz had originated in New Orleans' red-light district, with the word 'jazz' itself derived from a black American term for sexual intercourse. It wasn't coincidental. Dancing to jazz after years spent humming home-fires anthems or remembering tired, bawdy music-hall ditties ignited the souls and libidos of a generation eager to shake off the wartime blues. As well as the charleston there was the twinkle, the camel walk, the shimmy and the vampire to get one's bandy legs around, and in London, nightclubs, both licensed and unlicensed, flourished. While after-hours jazz clubs operated illegally, by 1919 the original Dixieland jazz band had played at the London Hippodrome. But despite the tidal wave of jazzmania as the *Daily Mail* monikered it, popular opinion as to whether it was terrific or tawdry remained divided, with the same paper pronouncing the charleston, 'reminiscent of Negro orgies'. When the Hammersmith Palais opened, one particularly irate clergyman announced, 'the morals of the pigsty would be respectable in comparison'. The government tried to quash it, to no avail.

London nightclubs weren't just places to drink and dance, but to enjoy cabaret and other kinds of musical entertainment. A 1923 law meant that music halls lost their drinking licences, making nightclubs the only option. When the Kit Cat Club opened in Haymarket in 1925, its membership soon swelled to more than six thousand, and included the great and good of society alongside everyday revellers who could afford the fees and drinks prices. It may not have been prime spouse-hunting ground, but it was certainly the place to flirt and find yourself an evening's lover in the meantime.

For the newspapers, a primary problem with the nightclubs was the fact they allowed black men and white women to dance and drink together. In 1924, police entered the Erskine Club in Whitfield Street, London – a restaurant and club that sold a variety of alcoholic beverages, allegedly without a liquor licence. But the real crime was the racial mix – the jazz band containing mainly black musicians, and the white women that fraternised with them and other black guests, dancing with them, and sitting on their knees.

When Nancy Cunard, a female bohemian artist made a play for 'negro artists', before embarking on an open affair with one Henry Crowder, it was to the embarrassment of high society – and it did not go unremarked upon. Lady Asquith, having lunch with Nancy's mother, Lady Cunard, one day, apparently asked, 'What is it now – drink, drugs or niggers?'

It would be the burden of another generation to make mixed-race relationships acceptable, not only to polite society but society at large. Meanwhile, across the rest of the country the dance hall became one of the most respectable venues – particularly if it was a church hall – by which to meet a potential mate. In the eyes of parents, it was far preferable a meeting place to parks or other open-air spaces where it was possible to indulge all too readily in sex before marriage, which was still heavily disapproved of, despite its relative frequency. Dancing was also relatively cheap – for a couple of shillings maximum you got a whole evening's worth of entertainment. Tea dances, held in the afternoons, were most popular with women, who would often dance with one another before the men arrived.

You didn't even need to be in Blighty to visit one. In 1920, a young soldier stationed in India wrote to the *Sunday Express*'s agony aunt, Gertie de S. Wentworth-James, lamenting his lack of a love life. He'd never had a sweetheart, he confessed, and was 'too shy to even talk to one of the fair sex without fear'. The solution, Wentworth-James advised, was to take yourself in hand, fixate upon the girl you fancied above all others, and 'set out to win her with all the dash and courage which you have hitherto expended on an attacking enemy' – by taking yourself off to a dancing class. 'If you do you'll soon "fox-trot" away your shyness and 'one-step' yourself into marriage!'

Besides, liberty had its limitations, as women struggling to hold down jobs and keep lodgings going were realising. In their droves women turned to magazines for advice about how to conduct their relationships. *Women's Weekly* agony aunt, Mrs Marryat, employed a kindly but candid approach in her responses. Replying to one letter from a poor young woman troubling over her and her husband-to-be's incompatibility when it came to sporting pursuit and whether she might indulge in her passion separately, Mrs Marryat concluded: 'I don't think you would have to write to me for advice if your love for your fiancé was the real thing.' Independence, it seemed, lasted only as long as your journey to the altar.

The official line was that flirtations versus relationships with a view to marriage required entirely different navigation, and expected entirely different behaviour from their relative participants. The single girl of the twenties could be short-skirted, short-haired, loose-limbed and lipped, smoking and drinking and career-focused; the future wife had to be accommodating and sacrificial.

My Weekly magazine proclaimed marriage 'The Best Job of All' and debated whether women should themselves propose. The conclusion was yes, on the basis that soldiers returning from the turgid horror of the trenches were too damaged to do it themselves. Meanwhile, the magazine *Woman's Own* recommended the kind of work that would help one catch a husband – namely working as a nurse, a library assistant, private secretary or telephonist, the latter particularly effective, given that 'many a man falls in love with a voice'.

What these magazines couldn't yet dare to do, however, was give the kind of graphic advice needed to really spark up the nation's physical relationships, even though such publications were eager to remark on the desperate need for that knowledge amongst the newly wed. Instead, it would be up to a thirty-seven-year-old virgin to bestow Britain with the answers.

When Marie Stopes published *Married Love* in 1918, it was effectively the first sex manual. Stopes wrote the book after being spurred on by the American birth control campaigner and speaker Margaret Sanger, and although initially turned down by a slew of publishers, it was reprinted five times in the first year when it finally did make the presses and, by the end of 1923, had run into twenty-two reprints and sold over four hundred thousand copies.

In her book, Stopes advocated the benefits of conjugal love, and physical pleasure within marriage. 'In my own marriage,' she told readers in the Preface, 'I paid such a terrible price for sex-ignorance that I feel knowledge gained at such a cost should be placed at the service of humanity.' Stopes should have known. When she had filed for divorce two years earlier, she is reported as saying of her husband's lacklustre penis, 'I only remember three occasions on which it was partially rigid, and then it was never effectively rigid.'

Of course, the information was just as applicable to unmarried love, even though Stopes would never say that outright (Stopes received letters revealing the real identities of single girls posing as married women, for example), and it's worth noting that she was vehemently and vocally anti-abortion. Yet she cared deeply about the plight of working-class women, and opened up the first birth control clinic in North Holloway in 1921 to tend to them as a result. Run by professional medical staff, the clinic gave out Stopes' 'Pro-Race' brand cervical cap along with advice. Despite just five hundred takers in the first six months, by 1930 the clinic had advised ten thousand women.

Her follow-up book to *Married Love*, *Wise Parenthood*, published in 1922, set out her views on contraception more radically and was widely condemned by the Catholic Church. Despite the British Social Hygiene Council realising that sexuality would probably be best taught during school biology lessons, government ministers ignored the Board of Education's recommendation in 1927 and it remained discretionary. Similarly, government ministers proposing that local health authorities should be allowed to give contraception advice didn't manage to convince the Ministry of Health until 1930. In the meantime, Stopes' books had a baffled, captive audience.

What's more, the number of letters Stopes continued to receive on a daily basis was a clear indication that plenty of arrangements outside 2.4 children existed, and that most people had no one but her to turn to for advice on them.

Take this letter from January 1926, from a woman whose husband had been locked up in a mental institution for nearly twenty years: 'I hope you will not judge me too harshly ... Nearly two years ago I met a widower, now the friendship has grown to love and I confess intimacy has taken place of late. How can we avoid an increase in family as it is impossible to marry as the law stands today?'

Yet here's where the public face of Stopes' compassion grew stony: she simply could not be seen endorsing extra-marital affairs and Stopes never replied.

And there was another group of women Stopes could not be seen to be helping, even though they also wrote to her expressing desire, longing and spiritual and emotional frustration: lesbians.

Doctors regarded 'failing in love' as women that might fall into excessive masturbation, short-lived affairs, or lesbianism. And if the 1890s had been the decade that exposed and condemned male homosexuality, then the 1920s was the decade that turned its attentions to lesbianism. It took the obscenity trial of a single book, Radclyffe Hall's *The Well of Loneliness*, to expose the Establishment's unease with female–female relationships. Besides the dictum that it was an 'obscene libel' and all copies should be destroyed, this was supported by a medical statement from Sir William Henry Wilcox, consulting medical advisor to the Home Office, stating: '[Lesbianism] is well known to have a debasing effect on those practising it, which is mental, moral and physical in character ... it is a vice which, if widespread, becomes a danger to the well-being of a nation'.

When MPs debated the Criminal Law Amendment Bill in 1921, they voted by 148 to 53 votes to criminalise sexual acts between women, with Lieutenant Colonel Moore-Brabazon explaining that 'abnormalities of the brain' were the cause of this libidinous disease, the only solutions being to ignore it, to lock up lesbians in asylums or to impose the death penalty on them. In the end, the House of Lords rejected the proposal on the basis that it would glamorise lesbianism and make it even more attractive to impressionable young women.

Women themselves took a more rational approach. The author Constance Long saw lesbianism as an inevitability of war, and their standing in for men: 'Something male in a woman's psychology has been called for, and we have seen there is a latent sex-element which enables her to respond.'

But the damage had been done. It was now impossible to be considered an upstanding young woman if you were romantically interested in your contemporaries. One woman who knew this more than most was the writer Vita Sackville-West, perhaps the most famous lesbian of the period, her own ambiguity towards her sexuality mirroring that of the era in which she lived.

Vita was herself married to a gay man, the writer and diplomat Harold Nicholson, who was aware of Vita's amorous proclivities – and her affairs. Seemingly slightly jealous of her most captivating lover, Violet Keppel, he described how Violet's will 'becomes like a jellyfish on cocaine' when she encountered Vita, who was herself equally infatuated with Violet. She cross-dressed, becoming her male alter ego 'Julian', and spent a blissful summer in Cornwall with Violet in 1918.

In doing so, she'd left two children behind and was soon reprimanded by her entire family for abandoning them. Vita returned to her family, and Violet, to whom she'd promised they would be reunited, went on to marry herself. Violet's obsession with Vita and her desire to elope ran right up until the day before her marriage, as evidenced by the letters she sent to both Vita and Harold. Forty years later they were still in communication. As the years passed, other women, including Virginia Woolf, took Vita's fancy, and she found some acceptance amongst the Bloomsbury set, but Vita never settled into her sexuality, despite her relative privilege.

What's more, when the seminal lesbian novel of the twentieth century, *The Well of Loneliness*, was published in 1928, Vita herself poured scorn on it, calling it 'trite', 'superficial' and 'loathsome', although apparently only on account of its poor literary merit. Nevertheless, the book was prosecuted under the Obscene Publications Act and banned in Britain until 1949. But Radclyffe Hall, the book's author, went on to receive some five thousand letters during its trial, mainly from gay women expressing their gratitude towards her for having dared to write it. As it turned out, the 1920s was actually boom-time for lesbian literature, with Virginia Woolf's *Orlando* and Elizabeth Bowen's *The Hotel* also hotting up the presses.

Also, although scant, there were venues for gay women to meet, namely private parties and salons, and the well-heeled women-only Forum Club. And in Paris there was the infamous venue known as Le Monocle, which attracted British lesbians from all over the country for a quick sojourn.

Gay men, meanwhile, could – and did – decamp to Berlin, where newspapers and clubs specifically dedicated to them could be easily found, and the first gay demonstration was held in 1922. While London's Piccadilly remained a hive of homosexual activity, pubs in Fitzrovia, the Bloomsbury set's heartland, were bohemian enough to accommodate those on the fringes of conventional sexuality, however they defined themselves. Liverpool, meanwhile, was known for its private parties and a venue called the 45 Café, while Cambridge held private dances and drag shows. Edinburgh, Manchester and Brighton were all similarly equipped. But the fact remained – the further you got from Bohemia, the more you took your life in your hands by chancing a face-to-face meeting.

It's no surprise that many gay men and women turned to euphemistic Lonely Hearts ads as a means of meeting a lover. But they were wrong if they thought it were a safer option. In 1920, an anti-prostitution campaigner called R. A. Bennett made a formal complaint to the high police commissioner about a plain-covered pamphlet selling in newsagents across Britain. Divided into three advertising sections – 'Ladies', 'Soldiers and Sailors' and 'Civilians', *The Link* was designed to help people find companions and friends of both sexes. Bennett's objection wasn't really to the concept, but to adverts such as these, from men looking from male friends: 'Lolaus' . . . '24' . . . of an 'intensely musical' and 'peculiar temperament ' . . . 'looking for many years for tall, manly Hercules'. Soon after, a man named Walter Birks was arrested in Carlisle on a charge of fraud before he was also found in possession of love letters from a 22-year-old Belfast-based clerk called William Ernest Smyth, and an ex-serviceman called Geoffrey Smith from Enfield. Charged with gross indecency, the three had met and corresponded through *The Link*. The magazine's founder, Alfred Barrett, was also charged.

When the case came to court, Barrett was found guilty of corrupting public morals, and of aiding and abetting his advertisers in a conspiracy to procure acts of gross indecency, with the three advertisers guilty of conspiring to commit it. The judge, Mr Justice Darling, chastised Barrett's publication 'for the purpose of allowing men and women to commit immorality' and sentenced all four to two years' imprisonment with hard labour.

This set a precedent. Publications were now wary of running Lonely Hearts ads at all, even if they were strictly catered to heterosexuals. But they didn't die out. In fact, given that there were fewer men to go around than women, and as the age of marriage increased – raising, in 1927, to sixteen for both men and women, from fourteen and twelve respectively – such publications only stood to benefit. Besides, the cost involved in finding, wooing and winning a partner was about to get even greater.

Chapter Seven

The Thirties: Monkey-walkin' from Mumbles to Mumbai

If the 1920s had been a time for jazzmanic dancing and mild courtship experimentation, the 1930s were the era in which the common populace began to 'settle down' again. As one Dr Cecil Webb-Johnson put it, 'The feverish time of unreflecting "war-marriages" has long passed though the consequences will not be overcome for some generations. People are more reflecting, and marriages of passion tend to become fewer.'

He also came up with an 'age appropriate' table for guiding matrimonial compatibility:

When the husband is aged:	The wife should be:
27	21
31	24
35	28
39	31
45	35
49	37
54	42
58	45

Although marriage rates among women had dipped during wartime and the early 1920s, the 1930s saw them buoyant once more. By 1931, the average age for marriage had fallen to twenty-five for women and twenty-seven for men, while the proportion of people marrying before the age of forty-nine had risen significantly between 1900 and 1930.

Still, poverty was a major factor in affecting dating and mating habits in the 1930s. It's no coincidence that 1933, the year with the lowest birth rate, was also the year with the highest unemployment rate. Men in particular were suffering. Without work, it wasn't only their livelihoods at stake. The blow to masculine pride left them morose and envious of any women who did have jobs. Not the best recipe for romance. Once upon a time, working-class parents had had good reason to force their children to delay marriage – if they were contributing to the household income then marrying before the age of twenty-five would severely deplete it. But by the1930s, this swung the other way, when means-tested benefits came into effect, and poor householders sought to reduce their income any which way in order to qualify for government income support.

Dating was a luxury few living through an economic depression could afford. Films may have fed romantic fantasy, but indulging your romantic desires was not necessarily the prudent answer, and women's magazines ruminated on the matter of marrying for love versus security. In the mid-1930s an insurance company called Britannic Insurance even sold a policy which offered protection 'in case you don't marry.'

But there were still ways to get your flirt on. If you were working class, the 'monkey parade', which took place on Sunday afternoons or summer evenings, was a chance to strut your stuff in your best threads before a bevy of local lovelies. While some single working women lived at home, many now lived in digs with a landlady, or in a small flat with a communal bathroom and kitchen, which released them from the scrutiny of why – and for who – they were putting on their best face and frock. The age of the chaperone was long over and it was perfectly possible to go to tea or dancing with a gentleman caller. Landladies could still exercise a matriarchal finger though, so sneaking a man back after dark risked your tenancy. On the other hand, there was a new generation of single ladies that would never have a ring put on it; by 1931, a third of the women who had not married by the age of twenty-nine never would.

In many ways that was bad for society but good for the economy. Some women in the 1930s actually married to ensure they'd never get called up to national service again.

Middle-class women, meanwhile, were advised to join a tennis club, take up ballroom dancing lessons or attend dances in order to meet a suitable young man.

The upper classes still relied on 'coming out' seasons, but to less effect than before, given the depletion of men since 1918; according to the 1921 census, there were 1, 720,802 more women than men, with the mortality rate for some reason higher amongst baby boys.

And if you couldn't find a man in England? There was always India. In the 1920s and '30s, young men and women that had been born in the tea and coffee plantations and shipped out to boarding school in England were returned to their unlikely homeland. For the men, this was an opportunity to do business. For the women, their chance to marry. These women were part of what came to be known as the 'fishing fleet' and some, such as a beautiful, spirited girl called Dulcie Hughes who was the daughter of the

Mayor of Marylebone, were even sent from London to the Raj as a last marriage-making resort. At twenty-eight, Dulcie was considered more or less past it on the London dating and mating scene so in 1934 she set sail for Colombo with her twenty-year-old sister Dorothy. One year and thirteen proposals later, she was on her way back to London, a 'returned empty' as the damning phrase had it. The reason she told her parents? 'They were either after my money or my body.'

For army families, time spent in India was the new debutante 'season', while women who had already suffered failed marriages, such as the 21-year-old Violet Hanson who had unwittingly married a homosexual, could be sent out to start afresh. And the hunt started on the boat, with many a young male passenger singling out an attractive woman before the hordes had a chance to get their hands on her. Sleeping out on deck was just one of the thrills for a young voyaging couple, although, as an eighteen-year-old boarding-school girl called Joan Henry returning to her home put it, 'kisses on the boat deck with the moon making a silver path over a smooth sea was as far as it went or was even expected'. And then there were the men already married, seeking a quick and discreet thrill on their return to a put-upon Penelope of a wife. A young woman called Cecile Stanley Clarke described how an older forty-something man had come to kiss her, which she put down to 'the phosphorus on the water' which had 'funny effects on the most sober of men'. Her conclusion? 'They can love one Woman with their Whole heart and at the same time get quite a lot of enjoyment from kissing another, and it is no good getting on one's high horse about it, it is just something to do with masculine hormones.'

Frequently, by the time the boat docked, the affair was over. Others used it as an opportunity to scope out potential mates for pursuit once they made it to dry land, with some starting courtships aboard that lead to more or less immediate marriage once they docked. This was encouraged by local Indian churches who did not approve of women 'loose' in India. Then there is the tale of an attractive 36-year-old named Kitty Irwin, who was invited to stay with a married friend in Karachi. During her six months 'on tour', she met an exporter called Sam Raschen who became more or less besotted with her at first sight. When she arrived at the booking office to arrange her passage home, she was escorted to see Raschen in his office at the dock and he subsequently persuaded her to delay her return indefinitely and, instead, marry him.

Risking it all for love would become a common theme of the 1930s. In 1936 came the abdication of Edward VIII, devoted as he was to American divorcee Wallis Simpson whom the constitution would not allow to become queen. It's hard to imagine the levity of the crisis these days, given the allowances the monarchy has made for Charles and Camilla, and the change to the primogeniture rule which would have made William and Kate's daughter Princess Charlotte heir to the throne had she been born before her brother George. If a strong monarchy depended on a complex tapestry of strategic marriages, Edward had just pulled on a master thread.

Of course, its broader message to the general populace was one of grand romance. Despite being a slinky American socialite, Simpson was not particularly popular with the public. But Edward was and, more importantly, so was the message that his willingness to forgo the throne for a life with Simpson imparted: marry for love, not duty, whatever your standing. All in all, the abdication was probably the most romantic episode in the royal soap opera since Queen Victoria proposed to Albert.

For gay men and women, romantic opportunities were also escalating. The year 1937 saw the publication of a book called *For Your Convenience*, a euphemistic guide to cottaging, which marked out the best kind of public toilets in which to meet 'like-minded' male cohorts. At around the same time, certain pubs in London became known for their queer credentials, places where both gay men and women could meet and date under the protection of a dogged status. The most notable pub of the era was the Running Horse in Shepherd Market, which had even seen the writer Radclyffe Hall drink there prior to the publication of *The Well of Loneliness* back in the 1920s. Gay men, meanwhile, didn't date so much as hook up rampantly. In the early 1930s, young working-class men would stand at the back of Collins Music Hall in Islington and masturbate one another, pick one another up under the arches of the Adelphi between Charing Cross and the Embankment and in parks London-wide, from St James's to Hackney Marshes. Meanwhile Lyons Corner House on the corner of Leicester Square saw gay men queue around the block to get in for tea and toast on a Sunday, with the code, 'Is she TBH (to be had)?' the way of marking out someone's sexual availability.

Police officers scouring the city for proof of gross indecency continued to make arrests in these areas of London, with officers routinely rubbing a suspect's cheek with blotting paper to test for make-up. For many men, who didn't strictly identify themselves as homosexual, this was just a way of getting a sexual fix when women were reluctant to put out before marriage.

And yet it was also in the 1930s that the divorce laws were amended, in theory making it easier than ever to end a marriage. Before 1937, adultery had to be proven in order for a divorce to be granted, which meant acrimonious but non-cheating couples had to orchestrate a 'visit' from a random lady friend or chambermaid to a husband's hotel room in order to fake infidelity. After the Matrimonial Clauses Act of 1937, however, the first major change to the divorce laws since 1857, annulment could be granted on the grounds of non-consummation, being of unsound mind, having epilepsy, venereal disease, or being pregnant by another man. Yet although ending a marriage no longer required a trip to the London Divorce Courts, it was still extortionately expensive and constituted reputational suicide. The fact that only ninety MPs turned up to Second Reading of the Bill which saw it become law indicates just how taboo divorce would remain. It would be at least another thirty years before the laws were amended again to enable either partner to divorce the other on the basis of the irretrievable breakdown of the marriage.

Given the costs to reputation and wallet, more people separated than divorced, and women's magazines waged a propaganda campaign to ensure that ladies nearly always held on, even in the most undignified of circumstances, to the man they had so fought tooth and nail to secure.

As the writer Winnifred Holtby put it, in *Time and Tide* in 1935, 'Today there is a far worse crime than promiscuity: it is chastity. On all sides the unmarried woman today is surrounded by doubts cast not only on her attractiveness or her common sense, but upon her decency, her normality, even her sanity.'

But there were other women ready to rescue her reputation. In 1937, Marjorie Hillis published *How to Live Alone and Like It*, an etiquette guide for the single girl. The book is funny, frank and disarmingly modern in its conclusions about life without the hassle of a husband, the key tenet of which seems to be learning not to care that one is alone in the first place. That's when the men come flocking – 'If all . . . refused to talk to a man, they would soon find suitors playing the guitar under their windows.'

The handbook exposes many of the contradictions of trying to live as an independent woman who suits herself, but who might want sometimes to invite the attentions of men. On the matter of hobbies, for example, Hillis is resolute: 'there was a time when a hobby was absolutely de rigueur . . . but hobbies are anti-social now; modern men don't like to be sewn and knitted at; and the mere whisper that a girl collects prints, stamps, tropical fish or African art is, alas, likely to increase her solitude'.

But when it comes to physical grooming, Hillis recommended that a lady groom for the good of her self-esteem in the first instance, enjoying its knock-on benefits in the second: 'The woman who always looks at night as though she were expecting a lover is likely to have several. (One of the pleasantest things about modern life is the increased range of suitors.)' Similarly, there's a whole chapter dedicated to alcohol, covering everything from how to arrange a mini drinks cabinet to how to avoid giving your friends hangovers when you're hostessing, the overriding conclusion being 'it's a wise lady who knows enough to confine her drinking to social occasions'.

On the matter of sex, the book was equally straight-talking. Automatically presuming that single women were indeed indulging their baser instincts, Hillis advised those who were to keep it to themselves: 'A Woman's Honour is no longer mentioned with bated breath and protected by her father, her brother and the community. It is now her own affair.'

While we're mentioning affairs, Hillis recommended they 'should not even be thought of before you are thirty'.

Similarly, inviting a gentleman friend to stay was perfectly acceptable. A woman should not be concerned with what the neighbours might say if they see him coming and going. Rather, the issue is what he – and you – might get up to if he does in fact stay the night – 'you probably know him better than we do, but it is our opinion that it usually takes two to make a situation'.

Women were allowed to invite men to events on the proviso that they develop a devil-may-care attitude about his attendance – 'the best rule is to make your invitations worth accepting and not to care what the man thinks so long as he comes'.

Although the Victorians had been keen on physical exercise and well-being, the 1930s saw the dawn of what would eventually become our fitness industry. Of course, it targeted women. In 1930, a 47-year-old widow called Mary Bagot Stack launched the Build the Body Beautiful League, soon to be known as the Women's League of Health and Beauty. Mollie, as she was nicknamed, devised a programme of classes in dancing, callisthenics and remedial exercise, and members of the league devoted fifteen minutes a day to healthy activity including walking, running, sports and indoor exercise. Members of the league could be any age, had to sign a pledge committed to regular exercise, were advised to shave under their arms, use deodorant and be sure to always have a clean handkerchief up their left knicker leg. The idea was to fit women's bodies for childbearing and rearing, and Mollie's programme was effectively the first aerobics workout. The league's emphasis on exercise for all, irrespective of class, struck a particular chord with inter-war women and in particularly deprived areas of Britain the class fee was waived. The men who lined up to watch them at the public workouts didn't complain either.

Meanwhile, men's bodies were also the subject of physical priming with the purpose of attracting women. In 1929, an internationally renowned radiologist called Alfred Jordan devised the Men's Dress Reform Party alongside a group of leading eugenicists who wanted to make the male body more beautiful. They countered stiff collars and starched shirt fronts, recommending hats be worn only as protection against the weather and that underwear should be non-constricting. Skin was to be as bare as possible, whenever possible, and tanned skin, formerly the preserve of peasants, the complexion ideal. They imitated a group called the Women's Rational Dress Society, which had been set up in 1881 to protect against clothes that might damage health or deform the figure, but their real concern was to reverse the decline in birth rate amongst the middle classes. As one of their members, Dion Byngham wrote in the *New Health Journal* of 1932, what they were aiming for was 'a renaissance of beauty for men – true masculine beauty of the body and mind, the bloom of a joyful spirit – might mean happier marriages, well-born and beautiful children, a healthier and more beautiful race'.

They were soon roundly mocked. In a lecture he gave at the Royal Institution about 'The Future of the Human

Race', one of the core members, W. R. Inge who was the Dean of St Paul's, predicted that in the future all men and women would wear a simple tunic with a cloak thrown over in cold weather. By 1937, the MDRP's backer was bankrupt and any dreams the men may have had about becoming a sort of 1930s cross between the Rat Pack and the Chippendales were in tatters.

Most men, meanwhile, continued to live and die by a good fitting suit: bespoke Savile Row for those who could afford it, Burton or Horne Brothers off-the-peg for those that couldn't.

Fashion for women, meanwhile, took on a more modest tone than the flapper fashion of the 1920s. In a 1930 edition of *Good Housekeeping*, an article on a new Parisian collection of longer calf-length skirts noted, 'Certainly it is much more comfortable than the very short one that made sitting down a cautious affair.' Men approved too: 'The average man thinks that the right length for a skirt is one that leaves the hem hovering about midway between the ankle and the knee.'

But the relationship between what women wore and whether contemporary men approved of it was becoming more complex. In an essay written by a male author for the magazine the same year, entitled, 'Do Women Dress to Please Men?', the criticism of flapper fashion that had held sway but a decade ago was waning. 'The majority of men like bobbed hair, even when they have a sentimental affection for long tresses,' it evinced, although there was a caveat: 'but no man can abide the contemporary habit of combing the hair in public'. Some fashions were still not acceptable. On the matter of long, red nails, for example, 'I have never met a man who was not utterly disgusted by this horrible habit . . . "They look like claws dripping with blood!" '

But women were kicking back. Make-up was still regarded by the older generation as a sign of sluttishness, but, in 1935, the average reader of *Good Housekeeping* spent £15, 1 shilling, and 3 pence a year on grooming. The war had rapidly changed attitudes to what women wore and, by proxy, what women could do. Reflecting on previous generations' criticism of tomboyish fashion in females, an article from the same year asserted '. . . it is a mistake to think, as do some of the Victorianly-minded, that the tomboy quality presupposes something freakish, abnormal, or, in the wrong sense, mannish'.

Given that women had been given the vote in 1928, fashion was merely reflecting an increased equality: 'They wear, if they choose, the same sports-clothes, drive the same cars, and smoke the same brands of tobacco. To say nothing of taking on the same jobs of work, and spending their leisure in the same places of amusement; where, from the back and down to the waist, the young of both sexes are often indistinguishable.'

But if in appearance women were aping equality, how was this impacting on their dating relationships?

The cover essay from a 1930 edition of *Good Housekeeping* held a clue.

In 'The Kind of Girl I Want my Son to Marry', the celebrated American writer Kathleen Norris explained how men that held on to the ideal of their partners as having the party-loving spirit of the 1920s was not doing much for long-term compatibility: 'Her breathless reverence for wifehood and motherhood mean nothing to him. To him, his wife is still just his favourite dancer, and the jazzing and speeding and spending and drinking and smoking and gambling are to go on, indefinitely, on just the old terms. And that primarily is why so many young marriages fail.'

While Marie Stopes had been fielding questions on sex for at least a decade by this point, the double standard surrounding male versus female liberty was in full force: 'Girls govern their conduct before marriage strictly by what boys demand; if boys want girls to be cuddlesome, irresponsible little kissers, some reckless girls reduce themselves promptly to the physical level' and yet, 'Sensible girls despise bare knees, baby talk, and the incessant sickening thought of sex, sex, sex.'

Of course, 'the physical level' and the thought of 'sex, sex, sex' was still propelling day-to day dating encounters. In the 1930s, the focus moved from the dance hall to the cinema as the prime location for a successful tête-à-tête.

In 1914, there were already three thousand British cinemas; by 1939 this had risen to five thousand. To put their ubiquity into perspective, Middlesex alone had 130 by 1939, and by the end of the decade, some twenty-three million people attended 'the talkies' at least once a week. In contrast to the dance halls, by the 1930s cinema tickets were discounted for the unemployed. And while the dance hall was still the best place to meet a potential love, the cinema was the venue in which to escalate and enhance the relationship.

The most popular films of the decade included historical romances such as *Queen Christina* and *The Adventures of Robin Hood*, romantic dance comedies such as *Top Hat*, and the bombastic *King Kong* – where a woman could feign fear and clutch at her male paramour for protection. The decade ended with *Gone With the Wind*, which would go on to become the highest grossing film of all time and afford courting couples nearly four hours' worth of time in each other's company – no wonder it was so popular.

But if cinemas were seen as places to smooch and sin in the dark, professional censors were keen to ensure nothing on screen should prove arousing. In 1930, the British Board of Film Classification released a report detailing just what it found to be unacceptable. Of the 191 films deemed objectionable, sexual and social content made up the majority, and scenes of 'vamping' men and women in bed together, semi-nudity and dirty dancing, brothels, free love, companionate marriage, birth control and abortion all met the cutting-room floor. Given the list of strictures, it's a wonder openly sexual actresses such as Mae West ever made British screens at all. Meanwhile, women were called to exercise their boycott of the saucier films: 'It is incredible that women, the cinema's best supporters, will for ever continue to take an interest in seeing themselves so ill-used, and when their revolt is reflected in lowered box-office receipts the day of the credible and natural picture "drama" will be here.' So reported *Good Housekeeping* in September 1930.

But while depictions on screen in the 1930s remained tame, books about sex – both titillating and educational – could be bought with increasing ease by mail-order catalogue. Contrary to what would happen in the decades to come, sex was a man's dealing and contraception assumed to be a male responsibility, although procuring it was still somewhat taboo. In 1938, the House of Commons passed a Private Member's Bill banning the display of contraceptives in all shops, instead allowing shopkeepers only the display of a sign of not more than a foot wide stating, 'Contraceptives sold here.' Circulars and advertising to the unmarried under-18s was also banned, 'except on request', noted a newspaper report at the time in the *Gloucester Citizen*. While there was great anxiety about the birth rate, which had fallen considerably since the war, knowledge about not only contraception, but conception amongst women, remained scant. In 1938, the Birkett Committee examining abortion found that many working-class women didn't know it was illegal, and abortificants, both effective and useless, with little information to help women discern between the two, were widely available. With the average age of marriage rising, it was obvious that people were finding ways to have sex whilst limiting its inconvenient procreative consequences, even if it was often a matter of trial and error. When the Family Planning Association adopted 'Children by Choice Not Chance' as its slogan in 1939, there were sixty birth control clinics established across Britain, including one in Belfast, and they were not only visited by married women.

Meanwhile, working and lower middle class women had even easier access to information about sex and relationships, heralded by a new wave of women's magazines: *Woman's Own* founded in 1932; *Women's Illustrated* in 1936; and *Woman* in 1937. Although the magazines focused on promoting an idyll of domesticity, they also ran a number of increasingly explicit articles on sex and relationships, with *Woman* featuring a series on the 'Psychology of Sex' and a test for frigidity. Books on how to have a happy sex life within marriage, in particular evincing techniques for mutual orgasm, boomed. In 1930, a title called *Ideal Marriage* by a Dutch gynaecologist called Theodore Hendrik Van de Velde went through forty-three printings. This was followed by *Threshold of Marriage* in 1933

– published by the Christian social purity organisation the White Cross, it sold more than half a million copies – then *Modern Marriage* by the author Edward Griffiths in 1935.

While the emphasis of these manuals was on pleasurable sex within marriage, and adultery, kinky sex, and non-heterosexual sex were not up for discussion, let alone recommendation, these books became universal hand-books for everyone wanting to improve their physical relationship, married or otherwise.

Even the diktat against masturbation was being relaxed and, by 1932, the Student Christian Movement had concluded that 'masturbation does no physical or mental harm'. The official line might have been how to improve marital love, but the anecdotal one was that this flood of sex advice benefitted those who were dating whether or not that were scouring for a life partner.

Still, how to enjoy a healthy physical and emotional life with someone outside of marriage remained a key topic of debate. While the philosopher Bertrand Russell argued against marriage altogether, believing that it crushed sexual relationships, the idea of 'contract partnership', first proposed by a eugenicist called Catherine Gasquoine Hartley back in 1913, began to take hold. The idea was that unmarried men and women could have children together, while the state provided insurance in the event of their break-up. It would circumvent all the problems created by needing to save for and organise a marriage, and give women more security than a standard free-love arrangement. From Hartley's perspective it would keep Britain racially fit, as well as maintaining the birth rate.

Others didn't think marriage should be thrown out with the baby and bathwater, and instead recommended a scheme of marriage education. Devised by a coalition of eugenic theorists, Christian groups, left-wing intellectuals and former social purity activists, so marriage guidance was born.

It may have been this renewed emphasis on solutions for engineering marriage that gave two of the decade's leading romantic entrepreneurs the best idea in the dating business yet.

In 1939, Mary Oliver and Heather Jenner, two lissom yet resolutely single 25-year-olds, set up what was to become Britain's most successful marriage broker company. For the upper classes, the wealthy and fashionable, it was a more efficient and organised version of the debutantes' season. In keeping with their high-class image, the pair rented an attic on Bond Street, decorated it as a fit-for-purpose office and named their organisation the Marriage Bureau. Within a month, the two women were receiving three hundred letters a day from prospective clients, as a result of glossy ads in high-society magazines and theatre programmes. They also drew notable press in the opening weeks, in both the *Daily Mail* and *Sunday Express*. Attracting everyone from football players to opera singers, and a notable number of middle-class professionals, they screened out undesirable clientele by setting the joining fee at a sizeable five guineas, with twenty guineas payable once the wedding vows were made. The Bureau was an instant success, and had something no matrimonial agency before it had – a decent reputation.

But for those that could not afford the Marriage Bureau's fees, there was a new broker on the scene: the threat of yet another wartime.

Chapter Eight

The Forties: Escaping knickers and GI games

If the First World War had taught civilians anything about how best to live their romantic lives, it was that now or never all too frequently meant just that. With no time for protracted courtships or long engagements, the whole nation effectively began to speed-date. 'It was here today and gone tomorrow,' as one girl serving in the WAAF during the 1940s put it, 'so I did not build up any long-standing relationships.' Yet curiously the marriage rate shot up. In 1940, there were 534,000 weddings in England and Wales, nearly 40,000 more than the previous year, and 125,000 more than 1938; Americans, meanwhile, married at the rate of a hundred a day during the weeks after Pearl Harbor. Brides were younger, with three in every ten under the age of twenty-one. If your days were numbered, best get all the amorous action you could in the bag while you had the chance.

The weekend affair – snatched romantic and sexual encounters spun out over forty-eight hours – was in many ways the prototype of today's Tinder encounter, albeit with further-reaching consequences, leading as it often did to a 'hasty' wartime wedding, before serving as honeymoon. Such weddings were very much in the make do and mend spirit of wartime. As a seventeen-year-old called Jean Taber of the ATS said on her marriage to a Canadian soldier, 'I felt very lovely at the time, but now I realise I couldn't have done in my ATS uniform, with my hair tied up with a shoelace. We had no civilian clothes so it was a khaki wedding with carrot tops and pinks from the garden as buttonholes.' Women often found themselves pregnant after one of these weekends and either stayed with an original husband or coupled up with someone else soon after, with many children being brought up by non-biological fathers. Babies born to married women were considered legitimate unless registered otherwise. In Birmingham, for example, almost a third of illegitimate births were to married women, a rate that was pushed up by the existence of American service camps around the area.

Once back at the front, couples depended, as they had during the First World War, on letter-writing to keep their relationship going. By 1944, more than 3 million airmail letters, 4.5 million items of surface mail and postcards, and 500,000 airgraphs were being posted every single week. But the delays to delivery caused serious psychological strife, driving some women back home to 'drift', as was the expression of the day, in order to forget about the love they presumed lost. And it was the same for the soldiers. A military psychiatrist posted in the Middle East reported that 'delays, irregularities or non-arrival of mail were potent causes of anxiety and depression even among the most stable personalities'. As such, the War Office began to take seriously the matter of transporting mail, and prioritised it whenever possible.

Just as the 1914 Defence of the Realm Act had instructed the authorities to check correspondence for the leaking of state secrets, so commanding officers began to read soldiers' mail home yet again. The tiniest bit of privacy was afforded by the 'green envelope' scheme, which allowed soldiers to put a certain number of letters aside each month to be read anonymously by the base commander, who would not know the sender. Still, it offered little in the way of freedom of expression, merely preserved blushes when a lonely soldier decided to share the frustrations of his heart (or loins) to his lady love. Couples that wrote overly passionate letters to one another could still have them censored or intercepted.

Romance was as important as sexual passion to many on the front line. If ever there were living examples of absence making the heart grow fonder, it was found in the private night-time reveries of men holed up at base camp, nursing their bundle of letters from the girl and stroking a faded photograph. Vera Lynn, aka the Force's Sweetheart, known for her sentimental style, was played more than any other artist, Americans included, on the radio at this time. Lynn even broadcast a show called *Sincerely Yours* that featured servicemen's request for songs.

Aside from the letters, what kept most relationships alive was the elusive 'leave'. It was not as insubstantial as we've been led to believe. Every three months of service gave a soldier seven days off, a day for travelling, plus an additional forty-eight hours, which could be added on to make ten days in total. Female partners were meant to secure leave for the same time, although it was invariably tricky and they often just skipped their work or duties instead, something to which the authorities frequently turned a blind eye, given that anxious soldiers were seen to threaten national livelihood. Soldiers posted overseas, meanwhile, could obviously not venture back home to take their sweetheart out to tea. Instead, they received two travel warrants a year, which was later increased to four towards the end of the war. For the authorities, leave was a necessary evil – all too often women tried to influence their lovers into staying longer, avoiding dangerous duties, or from accepting promotion which could lead to loss of allowances.

Across the pond, the notorious 'Allotment Annies' had a nuptial strategy of their own. Allotment Annies were women who roped departing soldiers into marriage in order to secure the $20 a month that the US government automatically assigned to servicemen's wives, $50 in the case of a private. If you were married to an airman, you also received a $10,000 cheque in the event of him being killed in action and some women, sizing up the high rate of pilot mortality, actually sought out airmen for this very reason.

Even if he were to survive, all this time away from your honey was to put a strain on all but the most robust of arrangements. Women's magazines were careful not to condone affairs, but they still emphasised the need for discretion and secrecy – no husband needed or wanted to know what slip-up you had made while he'd been busy fighting for King and Country. But the number of illegitimate births – which rose from 26,574 from in 1940 to 64,743 by 1945 gave the game away. Abortions of course were illegal and extremely difficult to arrange, although they did take place in private medical clinics or in the back streets, which all too frequently endangered a woman's life.

But not everyone dated and mated in such a full-on fashion. In London the 400 Club and the Gargoyle were never empty, and the Windmill, the Piccadilly revue club which featured nude beauties stood stock-still in inventive tableaux, famously never closed, whatever the air raid. Equally popular with men and women, the owners never underestimated the salubrious effects of alcohol and firm naked flesh, whatever the sexual orientation of their patrons. Community singing flourished in pubs and bunkers, giving strangers an excuse to crack at least a smile at one another, and the cinema continued to be a prime place of escapism, a darkened sanctuary where nobody cared whose hands were where for the duration of the show.

Frequently though, life in the time of air raids needed a more kinetic distraction. Dancing was once again the best way to boost one's spirits, and an excellent excuse to get your hands legitimately on members of the opposite sex. London's Hammersmith Palais and the Paramount in Tottenham Court Road staged jitterbug marathons and swing contests. The jitterbug was an import courtesy of the American GIs, which at first bamboozled Brits, but it soon caught on, despite an article from a 1938 edition of the *Daily Mirror* on the dance headlined, 'Why You'll Never See This Danced in Britain.' Meanwhile, chain dancing, conga-style, was popular for those who couldn't quite cut the prescribed shapes of the foxtrot or waltzing, which were also revived. Previous strictures on just what kind of dancing was appropriate were tossed out of the window, along with your inhibitions: you never knew when your turn on the dance floor might be your last.

Dressing up was also a crucial part of upholding public morale while boosting your sex appeal. For most working women, their daily uniform was entirely unbecoming, although many admitted choosing their service according to the uniform. In the ATS, for example, women wore a single-breasted, belted khaki jacket, with bulky pleated pockets, unflattering to the female figure, fitting 'about as well as a bell tent' according to one recruit. The uniform also required knitted knickers similar to long johns which women monikered 'twilights' and 'blackouts', and shapeless cotton bras. In factories, women were kitted up in the unbecoming boiler suit.

At the beginning of the war, stockings and make-up were still routinely available and on Friday nights, a typical young female factory worker could be seen prepping herself for the evening ahead in the toilets of her workplace. Lipstick was an essential, and mascara came in a solid case that you spat into then applied with a brush. Hair, meanwhile, was worn in curlers under a headscarf during the day, before being released for the evening, and stockings were put on in the mornings underneath boiler suits to save time. Topped off with the dress and shoes carried carefully in a paper bag and the girls were ready to go from factory floor to dance floor.

There was another reason dressing femininely was important; men did not trust women in masculine clothing, thinking it inspired in them 'masculine' traits of carousing, boorishness, and general sexual moral laxity.

As the war dragged on, rationing affected the availability of cosmetics and so women made do with sugar water for wave-set, Vaseline for eye shadow, shoe polish instead of mascara and starch instead of face powder. When the President of the Board of Trade announced in spring 1941 that clothes were being rationed, gravy browning began to be painted up the back of legs to imitate seamed stockings. A product called Silktona could be applied to legs to give the impression of sheen. Skirts became shorter simply because there was not enough fabric to go around. And then there was the issue of knicker elastic. In scare supply, women began to substitute it for buttons. Quite soon, 'escaping' knickers became a common sight in public, leaving many no choice but to step out of them on the streets before stuffing them in their bag. It makes you wonder why wartime women bothered with knickers at all.

Still, why give anyone an opportunity to question your sexual propriety? All women who signed up to the forces were given an STI examination and lectured about the negative consequences of having affairs. In 1941, Churchill set up the Markham Committee, allegedly to investigate amenities and welfare conditions in women's services, but really to serve as a way of checking up on their sexual activities. The committee was forced to conclude that servicewomen were no more promiscuous than the general population and a campaign to change public perception was launched. Meanwhile, the national STI statistics had increased by 70 per cent, and so many merchant seamen were reported infected in Britain's main ports that a Nazi plot was even suspected.

Yet if servicewomen could no longer be accused as the source of infection, they were still seen as easy and fair game, particularly by servicemen. While airforcemen tended to date Wrens and land girls, it wasn't unheard of WAAFs having to arm themselves with hat pins to avoid sexual assault. One WAAF even claimed that Polish soldiers stationed near to their base had bitten the nipples off some of her serving sisters, but out of rage or passion, it wasn't clear. From January 1942, all women at home were mobilised for the war effort.

They were crucial to victory but not always treated with the appropriate reverence. If anything, men actively discriminated against women because they found them so threatening to the status quo. Training was not invested in; it was taken as a given that women would return to the home once conflict ended. Women were given the easier 'clean' tasks for their own 'protection', and being groped or goaded was common. So much for old-fashioned manners.

At the same time, sexualised images of women were crucial to boosting wartime morale. Whether it was pin-ups, Hollywood stars, pictures of the girl back home or posters of female pilots, doing it for 'her' sake figured large in the soldier's imagination. Prostitution also grew exponentially during wartime and served many a function that dating might have done otherwise, providing men with fleeting companionship alongside sexual release and women, war widows or otherwise, much-needed extra income. In London, regiments of the so-called Piccadilly Warriors paraded their wares around a sandbagged area that had formerly displayed the statue of Eros, hidden away for the war.

But despite the permissive circumstances, many women remained exuberantly innocent. It was not until 1945 that sex education became part of the school curriculum, and even then it focused on the reproduction of plants, and other mammals if you were lucky. As Margaret Herbertson, a diplomat's daughter born in 1922, explained about sex, 'My mother said nothing at all about it to me. Zero. I had an idea that if you were married you had a baby, but how you had the baby I had no idea whatever. We were all very, very naïve.'

Still, even where there was little knowledge, sexual temptation got her talons in. Around 1940, the diary of a young woman called Joan Wyndham reveals her passion for one Rupert Darrow, her extremely handsome paramour, who one day asked, 'Would you rather I raped you in the proper he-man fashion, or will you tell me when you're ready?' 'I'll let you know,' she apparently replied, before noting 'inside me I could feel every moral code I had ever believed in since childhood begin to crumble away'. It's a too often trotted out cliché that war was an aphrodisiac, but there are numerous contemporary accounts to indicate that couples could actually be seen copulating in the underground during an air raid.

For gay men and women, an equally devil-may-care attitude prevailed. As well as wartime allowing for people who might never ordinarily meet to encounter one another, the issue of what the neighbours might say ceased to matter. As the man about town Quentin Crisp, who once described London as 'a massive double bed' during wartime, remembers asking a passer-by in London for directions, upon which the man 'kissed me on the lips, told me I was in Newport Street and walked on'. Others recall spending the night having sex in stranded railway carriages at Charing Cross Station; still others remember day trips to Brighton and Portsmouth, where a soldier known only as Barry, quoted in Peter Dennis' book, *Daring Hearts*, describes visitors from the navy as 'friendly, pleasant, amusing, ready to talk, some of them were ready for sex'. Meanwhile, for women wanting to meet women, wartime offered them similar opportunities, and in cities, including London, Brighton and Manchester, they found bars that catered to their sexual and social proclivities.

Personal ads still remained the safest way to meet if you were gay. While established papers such as the *Matrimonial*

Gazette, Matrimonial Times and *Matrimonial Post* began to fold, magazines such as *Picture Show*, aimed at fans of the big screen, were enjoying a boom-time and began to carry Lonely Hearts themselves. While its Star Fan Club column purported to offer straight couples a chance to connect over their favourite starlet, referencing a gay icon such as Bette Davis or Montgomery Clift helped send the right signal, despite homosexuality still being illegal. Ironically, and subversive though it may seem, overtly gay men found themselves relatively accepted at the front line, although they were often 'used' to ease the sexual frustration of their usually heterosexual comrades. Still, sex between men, if uncovered, could lead to court martials, with cases actually increasing during the war years, rising from 48 in 1939 to 324 in 1944.

Back on the home front, heterosexual women found partners of their own to 'use'. In 1941, the land army was joined by between two and three thousand Italian prisoners of war who had been captured by the British in Egypt, the first batch of whom turned up in Liverpool. Selected for their physical fitness, these virile young men attracted the attentions of the land girls left behind. As a young woman called Jocelyn Greening admitted, they had been prepared to hate the Italians, yet 'they were so handsome – black curly hair, shining eyes, little moustaches, square hands – that we soon found them impossible to ignore'.

The police fined girls who fraternised with them – a whole £10 – and local papers suggested that women who were even more familiar should, like women collaborators in France, have their heads shaved in punishment.

Then came the Canadians, who were frequently placed with families, with the entire corps of around twenty thousand occupying the Sussex coast from the summer of 1941 until 1943. Their general low morale, however – strapping young men that were in service but not seeing an ounce of action – did not make them the best bed fellows, although they did drink, carouse and crack on to the local women during leave.

And finally came the 'friendly invasion'. The year before D-Day might have well as been recast as 'G-Day', marking as it did the arrival of one and a half million GIs into Britain – and a much-needed bolster to the morale of Britain's women on the home front. As Madelaine Henrey put it, 'They brought into our anxious lives a sudden exhilaration, the exciting feeling that we were still young and attractive and that it was tremendous fun for a young woman to be courted, however harmlessly, by quantities of generous, eager, film-star-ish young men.'

'Overpaid, oversexed, and over here', the GIs were a breath of fresh transatlantic air with finances to boot. The average GI received £750 a year, compared with a British soldier's measly £100. With extra money earned for flying duty and overseas duty, many had never had as much money in their lives. If they were single, British girls were the spoiled recipients of their good fortune. Gifts included chewing gum, cigarettes, flowers, chocolate and sweets, tinned peaches and the much vaunted nylon stockings.

Many British women were so taken aback by the speech of the GIs that the military authorities even went as far as to prepare a pamphlet for the female staff of the NAAFI canteen to decode it: 'The first time that an American solider approaches the counter and says, "Hiya, baby!", you will probably think he is being impudent,' it pointed out. Comparably, American soldiers were given a pamphlet advising them on British customs, with the US Provost Marshal even going so far as to issue an extra leaflet entitled, 'How to Stay Out of Trouble' which naturally advised against sexual relations.

Of course the GIs and the land girls didn't heed it. British women loved the fact that the American troops danced, joked, and came armed with luxury food, stockings and make-up, and that they distributed sweets to any children they came across. GIs had charm and knew how to talk to women. British girls had lost their curves on a diet of rations but the GIs complimented their figures anyway. American GIs loved the fact they could exploit their 'exoticism', and that, compared to American women, English girls seemed happily passive, eager to please, and professionally unambitious. As one soldier put it, 'They [English girls] feel they can attain their goals by being easy on the nerves of their menfolk.' As Quentin Crisp, who was working as an artist's model at the time put it, 'it was the liberality of their natures that was so marvellous. Never in the history of sex was so much offered to so many by so few.'

In the early years of the war the GIs had been warmly invited by English communities, entertained courtesy of what were known as British Welcome Clubs. In a June 1944 edition of the *Newcastle Evening Chronicle*, a local entertainer of troops noted, 'The Americans here are young men and after a good time. They want a nice girl and a dance to take her to, a place where they can give her a meal, and a place to drink.' Soon the authorities realised the welcome needed to be a more civilised, organised affair and so the WVS and churches set up more than two hundred welcome clubs featuring pre-selected hostesses for that very purpose.

As the war progressed, the soldiers stepped out with local girls themselves, organising what were called 'liberty buses' or 'passion wagons' to transport the ladies to a dance at the US base. But such was the anxiety about the spread of VD that British girls started to be 'vetted' by the local city halls in order to attend dances. Indiscriminate soldiers continued to send unvetted passion wagons at any rate. Unfortunately, many a British girl swept off her feet by stockings and swing dancing could misconstrue a GI's intentions – the problem was that 'dating' as the Americans practised it had not yet caught on in the UK, despite the influence of Hollywood. Meanwhile the authorities colluded in keeping the GIs single. Permanent relationships and marriages were to be discouraged at all costs – it was thought that it would distract the GIs from their duties, and there was also particular concern that some might be indulging in bigamous marriages. In July 1942, President Eisenhower ruled that his men could only marry with the permission of their commanding officers, and the marriage had to be proven to enhance 'the interest of these European Theatre of Operations forces in particular and military service in general'. Marriage didn't even secure a British spouse US citizenship. In fact, the impending birth of an illegitimate child was one of the only reasons for allowing a marriage.

The off-duty pursuit of British women was considered part of the troops' 'rest and relaxation' and it was many a British serviceman's job to drive a truckload of rambunctious and horny GIs through a sleepy English village. A popular joke of the time ran, 'Heard about the new utility knickers? One Yank – and they're off.' Impromptu orgies or multiple sex with the one woman was also not uncommon; with a need to get back to base, seduction and foreplay had to be exchanged for lavish gifts. Soldiers could also be seen wearing coats in the height of summer which they used to wrap around themselves and their female partners during alfresco sex. And then there was the 'wall job' which necessitated no coat, just a firm vertical surface to press against, and which British women favoured, believing it protected them against pregnancy; the 'g-spot' by any other name.

But there was a threat to the GIs' sexual prowess – and that came in the form of more than one hundred thousand black American soldiers who found themselves stationed everywhere from Cornwall to Glamorgan. The British government had not wanted them to come to Britain at all – in fact the Conservative MP Maurice Petherick had warned Secretary of State Anthony Eden that their presence would result in mixed-race babies, 'a bad thing for any country' – but the government was overruled by the fact that President Roosevelt had sought to recruit one in ten to all aspects of the US military.

Black troops who arrived in East Anglia to build airfields were carefully segregated from white using a complicated rota system. Yet English women were as ready to dance with them as the whites, oblivious to the institutional segregation that formed a part of American military life, even if it was evident in small acts such as the ban on photographs taken of black soldiers dancing with white women.

But the white GIs soon sabotaged their fun, spreading rumours that the blacks carried knives and that they were out to rape all the women they encountered. They then openly fought with them over British women in the streets of Bristol, Preston, and finally Launceston in Cornwall in a battle over a 'black' and 'white' fish shop and black and white dances, reports of which the authorities were quick to quash. As a Home Office circular from 1943 read, 'the morale of British troops is likely to be upset by rumours that their wives and daughters are being debauched by coloured American troops'. What's more, under no circumstances were black GIs and white British women allowed to marry.

But as the author Barbara Cartland, once a WAAF welfare officer, observed, 'it was the white women who ran after the black troops, not vice versa'. Still, as the Woman's Own agony aunt Leonora Eyles explained, replying to a letter she received about friendship with a black soldier, mainstream society was simply not going to accept mixed race relationships: 'Although coloured people are just as good as white ones, you must see that marriage between you would stand little chance of happiness for either of you; his race does not like her, and her own people don't like him, friends are difficult to find, and if they have children they are often unhappy. I think you would be very wise to end the friendship.'

The trouble came to a head in 1944 when a 33-year-old woman from Combe Down near Bath claimed she'd been raped at knifepoint by a black GI she'd led along a path near her house after he'd called asking for directions. His counter-claim was that he'd already visited her previously and paid her for sex, which she now denied in order to save face, mainly because she was married. Whatever the truth of the story, when the case was heard, the jury thought it odd that she claimed she'd gotten out of bed where she lay with her husband and actively led the GI down the road, rather than merely point him in the right direction. Still, he was sentenced to death by hanging.

But when the case reached the papers there was a public outcry, and 33,000 local citizens called for his reprieve. He was let off and returned to his unit, but the episode remained a cautionary tale about sex and race in wartime Britain.

When the American troops left after D-Day, the US army postal service recorded that over a quarter of letters mailed by GIs from France during the first four weeks were posted to British addresses. Some twenty thousand British women had applied to be American wives. The transatlantic dating die had been cast.

But some women were left with more than just memories. Having a little adulterous fun may as it be, but finding yourself pregnant during wartime was the worst case scenario for any servicewoman, who would be duly issued a 'Para 11' and dismissed. Thankfully this is where the unbecoming uniforms could actually come in handy – hiding a pregnancy until the late stage was possible under the surplus folds of fabric, and being sent out to hospital with a case of 'severe constipation' one possible work-round.

As for those wives that had strayed, as Barbara Cartland noted, 'I was often sorry for the "bad" women ... They started by not meaning any harm, just desiring a little change from the monotony of looking after their children, queueing for food and cleaning the house with no man to appreciate them or their cooking.'

In fact, by the end of the war, so many couples had had adulterous affairs that one English bishop actually proposed a blanket pardon for all, given the unprecedented circumstances. The Archbishop of Canterbury couldn't agree, instead calling for a rejection of wartime morality, stating, 'People are not conscious of injuring the war effort by dishonesty of sexual indulgence.' It was at once attenuating and accusatory.

But it was also, in many cases, too late. Seven thousand nine hundred and ninety-five divorces in 1939 became more than sixty thousand by 1947. Publicly funded marriage guidance became ever important to the government and matrimonial agencies and friendship agencies flourished. By 1946, the National Marriage Guidance Council had been formed and reports on its regional units flooded newspapers. In an October 1947 edition of the *Gloucestershire Echo*, the Cheltenham Marriage Guidance Centre had noted that the chief causes of disharmony amongst those that had used the service were due to incompatibility, lack of cooperation, stress of modern life, long periods apart during the war years and unsatisfactory family background in childhood. Housing, mental illness and infidelity also featured. The solution, noted the local rector, was with the younger dating generation who 'were taking a more serious view of life than their parents ever had', and would find it nothing but normal to consult medical and counselling professionals should they ever run into trouble in later life themselves.

With women's reversion to their pre-war roles as mothers, wives and homemakers, they began to date with a cyclopian view to wedded bliss, and everywhere they turned, culture reflected this back at them. *Brief Encounter*, one of the most popular films of 1945, hammered home the message that it was time for women to turn their backs on romantic flights of fancy and instead step up to their spousal responsibilities. To be known as a 'bolter' was the ultimate insult.

With war over, their foreign lovers gone, and a new conversation about marital bliss opening up, the best thing to do was to embrace peace time, be thankful for your risqué memories, and focus on the fact stockings would soon be readily available once again. After all, what more could a woman facing the 1950s want?

Chapter Nine

The Fifties: Gentlemen prefer condoms

'You've never had it so good,' assured Prime Minister Harold Macmillan at a Conservative Party Rally in Bedford in 1957. But at the beginning of the decade, life in England was still relatively threadbare, with some wartime rationing still in place, an income tax rate of nearly twice of today's, and a make do and mend attitude prevailing. Whatever spoils you'd imagined the end of wartime would bring, if you'd danced yourselves dirty or made out until the lights went up in the picture house, you were still resigned to doing that until at least 1955. There simply wasn't the money for most people to do anything else.

But despite the relative austerity, dating, if you were a man, was an expensive business, albeit one that got cheaper after the first date. As the *Daily Mirror* reported in 1956, the average first night out cost £1 – that covered two cinema tickets, a meal, chocolates and the bus fares home. As ever it has been for men, that initial investment was a risky business and not one proven to have the right results. One William Chatters, twenty-four, of Cricklewood, a window cleaner, was resentful for having spent 'thirty quid on a bird over Christmas. And got nowhere.'

The notion of blind dates first appeared around this time. The preserve of country life, the paper reported that in Devon's Coln Valley, youngsters cold-called telephone boxes in the hope somebody would answer whom they could then take on a date. According to the report, 'They exchange descriptions of each other. If they like what they hear they get together.'

But for kids in the city, the dance hall remained the prime dating venue.

In his autobiography, *Free Association*, playwright and actor Steven Berkoff wrote in punch-drunk detail about his teenage turns at the Mecca, the Tottenham Royal dance hall.

As he recalls, 'Every night at the Royal was a dream time. You walked as if in slow motion and got there early so that you stood a good chance of pulling some sweet, delectable creature, had a good dance and swanned around. The dance was all-important since this was a way of demonstrating your skill as a mover, your grace, wit, balance and tricks. The jive was one of the greatest dance forms ever invented. And so all your arts were in some way fulfilled. You were the dandy, the mover and performer in your own drama, the roving hunter and lover, the actor adopting for the girl the mask of your choice. You wore your costume and walked the hall beneath the glittering ball and when you saw someone that you felt was about your stamp you asked her for a dance; if it was slow, when you took her on to the floor your heart started to increase its beat . . .'

At the beginning of the 1950s, the pop charts were dominated by artists such as Frank Sinatra and Tony Bennett, Doris Day and Ella Fitzgerald, who sang swing tunes and were accompanied by string orchestras. It had been a long time coming but swing dancing was just about considered civilised. But in November 1955, Bill Haley and the Comets hit number one with 'Rock Around the Clock' and changed the direction of dance music more or less overnight. When Elvis reached number two in the UK charts with 'Heartbreak Hotel' the following year, the future of dance music was cemented: it was 'stomping emotional music', as the *Daily Express* put it, which caused riots in cinemas wherever the film *Rock Around the Clock* was shown (police actually stood in the aisles to stop young viewers getting up and dancing).

What's more, the way people thought about love was also about to be indelibly influenced. The pace and energy of rock and roll had a direct impact on the lyrics being penned to accompany it. Lyrically at least, lovelorn longing was out, short-term sexual kicks were in. And the energy of the music was enough to attract young people in their droves, whether they danced or not. As Trevor Creaser, a teenager growing up in the 1950s recounts, 'you could take a pack of cards and play pontoon. That's what we did, although we really went for the girls.' By 1959, the dance hall was the most popular place to meet, with one in four couples finding love amongst the high kicks and card-playing, according to a Gallop poll of that year. Whatever the initial fears, the invention of TV seemed to have done nothing to dampen enthusiasm for it. After all, as a gentleman called John W. Waterfield writing to the *Daily Mail* in 1957 pointed out, 'You will not find a wife (or husband) by staring at TV every night.'

Interviewed for the *Daily Mail* in 1992, a working-class girl florist from Wood Green, London, recalled 'My first boyfriend was Kenneth Nash, whom I met at an open-air dance in a local park. They'd regularly set up a stand and the entire family would go and dance to the big bands. Kenneth and I had our first kiss walking home from one such dance. We'd stand on the doorstep talking until my father came out and said, "Isn't it time you got home, son?" '

Younger teens frequented youth clubs and cafés where a jukebox took the place of a band, blasting out the latest rock and roll hits, as the former MP Neil Kinnock recalls. Italian cafés, where people also savoured their first cappuccinos, were similarly important: 'I used to go to one of them and I remember the owner had a sensationally beautiful daughter called Nora.' Otherwise, cycling and picnicking, youth hostelling and an annual seaside holiday formed the backbone of everyday Brits' social and romantic lives.

As ever, Hollywood offered up a narrative alternative. Suddenly the sex symbols on offer were not carbon copies of one another. Actors ranging from James Dean to Marilyn Monroe, Audrey Hepburn to Cary Grant starred in roles that gave their characters complicated amorous escapades. Happy ever after might still have been the desired outcome, but that still left plenty of room for an erotic adventure or three along the way.

What's more, the growth of celebrity gossip in newspapers meant the off-screen 'relationships' of these stars were now regularly revealed in the tabloids. In a 1956 edition of the *Daily Mirror*, the actress Natalie Wood disclosed details of her friendships with James Dean and Elvis Presley. Of escaping to the cinema with Presley, Wood said, 'We had to sit in the front row so nobody would see us. Elvis would put his arm round me and I'd put my head on his shoulder just like all the other kids there.' This intimate style of reporting worked in two ways – it bonded the stars to the readers by appearing to be revelatory (even if it was in fact studiously choreographed and censored) while mimicking their own relationships. For the first time the gap between the star and the viewer was closing as the studios realised that proximity to celebrity rather than distance was what sold cinema tickets and 45s.

Many of the films on offer also depicted class-straddling love affairs. Take *Roman Holiday*, staring Audrey Hepburn and Gregory Peck, about a princess that hides her high-born status for the day to venture out with a lowly reporter, or *How to Marry a Millionaire*, featuring Marilyn, Betty Grabble and Lauren Bacall as three ladies on the lucrative husband-hunt.

These films ignited the English imagination, mainly because social mobility was still incredibly limited. Then again, there was also the rare case of life imitating art. In London, a provincial-born Birmingham lass named Norma Turner had made her debut as a dance hostess in 1924, which required her to take a turn with any duke, earl, knight or young millionaire who asked. Over the next couple of decades, she went on to meet and marry first Clement Callingham, the elderly chairman of Henekey's wine importers, before moving on to the 69-year-old Sir William Collins, another company chairman, before moving on again to Sir Bernard Docker, chairman of Birmingham Small Armaments, one of the largest British companies at the time.

Turner's champagne-soaked shenanigans were celebrated in the mainstream press, partly as proof that the end of austerity was nigh, but also as a means of entertaining a large female readership who couldn't get enough of her rags to riches escapades. When it came to comparing her behaviours with those of Hollywood movies, she was praised for using her femininity rather than her inherited wealth to achieve her goals of personal happiness and future security.

But it wasn't as easy for all female icons in love in the era. Take Princess Margaret, the original People's Princess. She changed what she wore according to fashion. She embraced Dior's 'New Look' despite feminist protestation, and at nineteen she was seen out in public smoking from an ivory cigarette holder, which would become her trademark. When she was photographed wearing a two-piece bathing suit on royal tour in Italy, the pictures winged their way around the world. It was the first time a royal had ever been photographed in their swimwear.

In fact, to be part of Margaret's circle was to be part of the Princess Margaret 'set', which included Jewish American entertainers, Guardsmen and men about town such as the old Etonian Billy Wallace, Mark Bonham Carter and the Marquess of Blandford.

And to occupy a round of clubs, which included the 400 Club in Leicester Square, the Milroy Club in Park Lane, and the Café de Paris near to London's Theatreland, perhaps the most famous nightspot of the period, where the Princess was often to be seen singing around the piano.

But Princess Margaret's life was chequered. As much as hers was a life of extreme privilege, her love life was disadvantaged and she was not allowed to marry the man to whom she was devoted, Captain Peter Townsend, because he was divorced. In fact, the only conditions upon which she could marry him were if she were to renounce her place in the succession, her title, her place on the Civil List, and subject herself to exile abroad for the rest of her life. Years later it turned out that both she and the Queen had been misinformed by the government and she would have been able to keep her title and money. But the wounds from Edward VIII's abdication were still open and Margaret was forced to atone for her uncle's sins.

Announcing their break-up to the nation, Margaret emphasised how this notion of duty had forced her hand:

> I would like it to be known that I have decided not to marry Group Captain Peter Townsend. I have been aware that, subject to my renouncing my rights of succession, it might have been possible for me to contract a civil marriage. But mindful of the Church's teaching that Christian marriage is indissoluble, and conscious of my duty to the Commonwealth, I have resolved to put these considerations before any others. I have reached this decision entirely alone, and in doing so I have been strengthened by the unfailing support and devotion of Group Captain Townsend. I am deeply grateful for the concern of all those who have constantly prayed for my happiness.

When she finally married Antony Armstrong-Jones, later known as Lord Snowdon in 1960, it was rumoured to be only because Townsend had himself married, thus breaking a promise that they had made one another to remain single. Despite two children, the marriage fell apart, as did Margaret's looks and reputation and Margaret's story became a cautionary tale. What's more, a national Gallup poll found that 71 per cent of the British public believed she should have pleased herself.

But you couldn't get too radical. In a newspaper report of 1954, the *Daily Mail* triumphantly reported on the failure of a marriage between two young communists who had been 'bitten by the Communist bug', professed free love and moved into a commune in Earl's Court, only for the wife to want out, upon seeing the errors of her ways, which may or may not have been prompted by the husband deciding he was not in fact a communist but an anarchist instead. The conclusion of the commissioner at the helm of the divorce hearing was that 'at the time of the ceremony neither had any respect for the marriage institution'. Divorce was still heavily frowned upon but making a mockery of marriage was even more severe. When, in 1956, the Morton Commission on marriage and divorce was set up in order to examine the possibility of a seven-year separation clause, the Commission simply couldn't agree and it would be another decade before reforms were introduced.

In 1955, the author Geoffrey Gorer published a book called *Exploring English Character*, a survey of some eleven thousand Brits' opinions on love, marriage, family, class, race and economics, based on answers sourced by the *People* newspaper.

Despite conservative anxieties about the decline of Christian morals, and the inhibition-loosening effect of two world wars, Gorer found that 52 per cent of the population were against any sexual experience for young men before marriage, 63 per cent of them against it for women, with the main reason given being that marriage should herald a new experience. That said, in the 1950s, three out of every one hundred men still lost their virginity to prostitutes.

Across the United States, Europe, Australia and New Zealand, young men and women seized the opportunity to tie the knot. Although just about sold on the American concept of teenage dating, by the age of twenty, six out of ten British girls were thinking about marriage, reported the *Daily Mirror* in 1959, with the average age endemic worry set in about it being seventeen. A steady relationship could survive a year, but if marriage wasn't proposed by that point, the girl was liable to lose interest.

In reality, the average engagement lasted two years and usually led to the Big Wedding – no comparison to today's bank-account busting affair, but the kind where dress, hosted guests, cake and wine were finally no longer rationed – could once again be afforded, as could setting up house away from parents, which prior to this had been prohibitively expensive and had meant it often took couples many years before they could ever have sex in private. The average age of marriage also fell – to 22.6 for women and 25 for men, the lowest it had been since the nineteenth century. Despite more women entering the workforce, the message being spread by the Establishment was that women should leave their jobs to tend to hearth and home. A wife should ideally support her husband's chances for capitalist advancement, while focusing on raising healthy babies.

What's more, this time around, there was no suffragist backlash to detract from the glories of domestic bliss. In France, Simone de Beauvoir's book *The Second Sex* may have sold twenty-two thousand copies in its first week but the response to its message was overwhelmingly negative. Instead, a light-hearted BBC radio debate from a May 1950 edition of *The Light Programme* better captures national attitudes. Quizzing four men on whether they thought husbands should have more than one wife, the framing of the question along with the remarks from guest WP Matthew were telling:

If you've got a kind of specialist wife, and she keeps the house very clean . . . but she has a face like the back of a cab . . . doesn't know a thing about literature, and calls a tennis racket a tennis bat then I think you have a perfectly good case for having three other wives . . . one a terribly good looker, one a sports fanatic and one a bluestocking. But if you've got an all-rounder then make do with her.

By the end of the decade, a programme on young people's views on sex and marriage found that fewer than ever were in favour of the institution, instead believing, as one interviewee who didn't want to marry put it, that 'sexual relationships with people is OK . . . I think it's stupid this virginity until you're married. I think it's terribly Victorian and if I'm sufficiently fond of a boyfriend, I think it's perfectly OK to sleep with him.'

A second female interviewee expounded:

When I'm about twenty-four, twenty-five, I hope to get married. Nice ordinary man and live in a nice little house and raise a family. I want to do everything I want to do before then though so that I don't have any regrets about being tied down. I don't believe in sleeping with everyone you meet but you meet someone and you're crazy about them so you go to bed with them and that's that. Don't be TOO easy though . . .

Easy or not, at least having safe sex was now an increasingly viable option – and one that pockets of polite society were willing to discuss, helped in part by the publication of the Kinsey Report.

Amongst American sexologist Kinsey's findings were the revelatory numbers of men and women that had enjoyed same-sex experiences, the comparative strength and pleasure of vaginal versus clitoral orgasms, and the introduction of a sliding scale of homo to heterosexuality. When the report was published, it had a significant cultural impact on both sides of the Atlantic. In a *Daily Mirror* article from August 1953, one of Kinsey's more controversial findings, that a woman more likely to 'neck' or 'pet' was also more likely to marry, was given a double-page spread.

If the revelations were meant to be shocking, the paper may have been underestimating the open-mindedness of its audience. Geoffrey Gorer's 1955 survey might have found an overwhelming distaste for premarital sex but it turned out to be class-based. In contrast to their middle-class counterparts, working-class men and women were confident enough to go on record saying they believed premarital sex was good for both men and women.

Britain, meanwhile, had its own 'Little Kinsey' report, born out of a controversial research project called 'Mass Observation', which collected data from designated volunteers about themselves and other people they effectively spied upon. Amongst its findings were the revelations that one in four men confessed to having visited a prostitute, one in five women had admitted to an extramarital affair, and about equal number of men and women had enjoyed a same-sex experience. Then again, it also revealed the scale of sexual ignorance. Take venereal disease. Most of those surveyed had no clue how it was caught, believing it was down to sharing towels and toilet seats, even by touching the same handrail as someone suffering from it.

If the 1930s and '40s had seen an increasing amount of sex education available, packaged as advice for married couples, the 1950s was ready to admit that the non-married were getting it on too – and prepared to give them candid, practical advice about how to navigate the vagaries of premarital sex in the process. In 1952, Leonora Eyles published the boldly titled *Sex for the Engaged*, in which she addressed all kinds of prickly social issues outside of the mechanics of sex itself, including whether one should 'marry out of my own class?' (the problems arising from not doing so being mainly different standards of cleanliness and attitudes to hat-wearing).

Desire, it turned out, was the core problem, particularly adolescent desire, which made being a teen 'not the best time to choose a life partner', and could lead instead to a second marriage being happier than a first when a young person previously led by desire learned to value other traits. As such, Eyles made a range of recommendations for dispelling youthful sexual energy, including swimming or dancing, as long as it was sober: 'I'm sure if there were more dance halls without alcohol there would be less sexual trouble among the young.'

Elsewhere, Eyles' general advice on how to have a happy relationship was actually pretty sound, even by today's standards:

If you want to have a really happy time in your courting, to remain a friendly human being, to keep intelligent and interested, and to lay the foundations for a happy home when you are married, make up your minds to encourage each other's interests, not to kill each other's friendships, to have two or three evenings a week apart no matter how much you dislike it; in fact, to respect each other's individuality.

But that's where the progressive viewpoint ends. As well as 'most of us having a guilt complex about sex', sex, as far as Eyles understood it, was a game only the male could really win. 'The male is the initiator, the female the conserver.' Eyles asserts at one point, that 'few men, however advanced and broadminded, [. . .] can endure to hear about a woman's sexual past' and that once men have had sex with a woman, they are more or less done with her, 'unless he has known her very well and got very friendly with her. But usually even then, he does not marry her.'

She also states: 'The YOU knows by instinct promiscuity is a mistake because it is a step back in evolution; animals have not yet learnt to be selective.'

Even a stolen weekend in a hotel could lead to disappointment for the engaged couple that embarked upon it – utilitarian pine furniture, a gas meter that needed a shilling you didn't have, all overshadowed by the fear of being found out.

Here, finally, was an antidote to that Victorian reasoning for a long engagement:

A long engagement is an almost hopeless thing; kisses, caressing, the rousing of emotions should have their natural consummation in intercourse. Again and again passionate lovemaking has to be arrested midway and both young man and young woman wonder why they are getting nervy, why their precious snatched hours degenerate into squabbles, why in the end the engagement just drifts into indifference or the man clears off to make a hurried unconsidered marriage with someone else.

But if there was one positive message from Eyles' book, it was that, even in these pre-Pill years when marriage was the usual answer to unwanted pregnancy and back-street abortions were still rife, birth control was increasingly accessible, which probably also helps to explain why the illegitimacy rate had gone down by this point. The NHS had been founded in 1948 and by 1955, the Minister of Health, Ian Macleod, had announced his support for the Family Planning Association. Soon, clinics up and down the length of the country were routinely dispensing diaphragms and condoms.

Making the point that coitus interruptus was rarely safe, Eyles was one of a bevy of writers helping to distribute scientifically sound and reliable information about sex and reproduction amongst everyday men and women. With this, plus the American concept of 'going steady' now in their armoury, the prospect of dating for its own pleasure rather than the mere prospect of finding a spouse was just about propping its bosom above the parapet.

But while commerce had learned how to appeal to a post-war desire for vibrancy and glamour, 'good girls' were still diligent, quiet, conscientious and, most importantly, modest. In an essay published in *Reader's Digest* in 1950 on the relative value of beauty, the author cited contemporary academic research from the University of California explaining the negative effect of 'extreme pulchritude' on teenage girls. Of six hundred girls surveyed, the more beautiful ones scored significantly less highly in their schoolwork than the so-called plainer ones. The conclusion? 'The most beautiful girls are apt to be disturbed by social engagements' which, in turn, made them more likely to drop out of university and so become 'selfish, at loose ends, and a very poor marriage risk for anybody'.

Whatever the movies might suggest, the idea that a woman who recognised the bargaining power of her beauty was a liability was the take-home. After all, concluded the article, 'the prime basis for lasting attraction is the deep-rooted desire to want to give, to want to please'; being beautiful – and knowing it – was not good for anyone.

It would be another decade before Hugh Hefner managed to convince the world that looking like – or bagging yourself – a *Playboy* model was something worthy of aspiration. In the meantime, women were torn between aping Marilyn Monroe in *Gentlemen Prefer Blondes*, shrink-wrapped in fuchsia silk and dripping in diamonds, and Princess Grace at her marriage to Prince Rainier of Monaco, daintily veiled and pristinely clad in prim white lace. What look would attract the better husband?

Men had fewer options. They were not meant to look pretty. They were meant to provide. So while the rebel of the era may have rocked denim most men's day-to-day dress was pretty drab – shirt and slacks at home, with a cap out and about for working men, or a rigidly shaded suit in charcoal, black or navy for business. Male dress meant business, and business meant making money and building a nest egg.

It was gay men that were to do something radical with fashion.

In London, gay and bi men about town had begun to adopt neo-Edwardian dress. In contrast to the double-breasted suit of the day, it created a neat, tight silhouette, with its fitted single-breasted jacket and slim-fitting trousers emphasising lean torsos, strong legs and firm backsides.

Finally, here was a way for queer men to carve out their own distinct identity without risking physical violence for it. By the 1950s, most major towns outside of London had at least one lesbian bar, often a venue shared with gay men, but increasingly a unique joint they could call their own. Brighton, by this point, had a visible gay and lesbian population at large, as well as a flourishing bar scene, which consisted of many tiny venues with couches and one corner bar where people would drink until sodden before moving on to the next place. Meanwhile, the British Legion Club was known to be particularly popular with middle-class lesbians, thereby illustrating the class divisions that cut across gay culture during the period.

But tolerance towards homosexual men was still luke-warm and sociological studies with titles such as *They Stand Apart: A Critical Study of the Problems of Homosexuality* and *Society and the Homosexual* illustrate the clinical separation with which they were approached. In murder and assault cases, gay 'provocation' was emphasised as justification for a physical crime and arrests in England and Wales for sodomy, gross indecency and indecent assault had risen from 719 in 1938 to 2504 in 1955. Dating as a gay man could simply not be done in the open. But a subtle allusion to one's alternative sexuality was just about allowed.

At the same time, the 'Teddy Boy' appeared on the scene. He was a macho, sometimes violent, working-class young man who had also adopted the flamboyance of Edwardian-influenced dress, marking himself out as being part of what was effectively the first post-war youth culture – and a rebel to boot. Teddy Boys occupied cafés, pubs, and milk bars, dressed in their drainpipe trousers, a multi-pocketed and draped jacket in full Edwardian style, with a moleskin or velvet collar. Shirts were topped with waistcoats, and a black knotted string tie known as a 'Slim Jim'. The look was finished off with a pair of brothel creepers. Their look even spawned a female 'Teddy Girl' equivalent, who wore a combination of male and female imitation Edwardian dress, still featuring broad, structured jackets in rich fabrics, Slim Jims, and either tapered trousers or calf-length, fitted skirts.

Although Teddy Boys attracted women in their droves, their costume was not worn to be sexually enticing, but to assert a new kind of working-class male authority. The style became synonymous with danger when a fight broke out among rival South London gangs, split between Teddy Boys and their regularly dressed counterparts, leading to the lethal stabbing of a seventeen-year-old bank clerk called John Beckley in 1953.

They were also fundamental in policing sexual relationships between white women and the new generation of Caribbean immigrants that had taken up residency in West London.

Mixed-race relationships weren't new to the 1950s. But a ruling in 1950 by UNESCO concluding that there was no biological danger in races intermarrying and having children together, plus the welcoming of immigrants from the Commonwealth to build a stronger Britain, marked by the arrival of SS *Empire Windrush* in 1948, made for a more welcoming climate. It's worth remembering that while racial segregation did not in any way rival what existed in the US, discrimination on the basis of race was not yet illegal. It was still common to see 'no blacks or Irish' signs in the windows of rental accommodation, for example, and even some dance halls still operated a colour bar, leading to an MP called John Baird to oppose the licence renewal of Wolverhampton's

Scala Ballroom in 1958 because it banned black men and women from entering. Yet at the same time, up and down the country, black, Asian, Chinese and white citizens were living side by side – and they were falling in love.

In 1953, the society wedding of the year was between Peggy Cripps, daughter of Labour MP Sir Stafford Cripps and a black Ghanian chieftan's son, Joe Appiah. Mixed-race relationships were settling across all classes, but when the wedding pictures were syndicated across the world, they caused outrage.

What's more, a poll taken by a North London vicar and sociologist, Reverend Clifford Hill, at this time found that more than 90 per cent of those surveyed would not approve of their sister or daughter marrying a black man.

London may have been the most multicultural city in Britain, but it was harbouring a distinct seam of racism, which was about to rise to the surface in a particularly unpleasant way.

In August 1958, a white Swedish woman called Majbritt Morrison was verbally and physically assaulted by a gang of white youths after she was seen arguing with her Jamaican husband Raymond Morrison in London's Notting Hill.

Besides throwing milk bottles at her and calling her 'black man's trollop', she was even allegedly hit in the back with an iron bar. Later that night, a mob of some four hundred, mainly Teddy Boys, began to attack the houses of West Indian residents in the same area, and rioted every night until 5 September. The police arrested both black and white perpetrators alike, until nine white youths were made examples of, fined £500 and sentenced to up to five years in prison.

But it wasn't only the Teddy Boys who objected to inter-racial coupling.

At the time of the riots, a Gallop poll found white citizens to be overwhelmingly opposed to mixed marriages. Around the same time the British National Party and Oswald Mosely's Union of Fascists campaigned against white/black sexual relationships. They tapped into fears about West Indian pimps controlling white women in West London, and drummed up fear across the country.

Meanwhile, the debate about the morality of homosexuals had reached tipping point. In the autumn of 1953, the young aristocrat, Edward Montagu, was arrested on charges of gross indecency, along with friends, Peter Wildeblood and Michael Pitt-Rivers, and sentenced to twelve months in prison. In many ways the case was a show trial – an opportunity for the authorities of the age to question the lifestyle of the man about town, and to question society's attitude towards gays. It was partly these events that would lead to the Wolfenden Committee being held in 1957, which would in due course lead to homosexuality being decriminalised in England and Wales, besides establishing a valuable precedent for all relationships, whatever your sexual orientation – that what you did in the privacy of your own home was your business.

In the meantime, the conversation about how most heterosexuals met opened up. By 1959, the *Daily Mirror* had launched a 'teen page', which featured problems answered by an agony aunt called Mary Brown. In May 1959, the topic turned to readers' stories of dating – how they'd met their beloveds, where they liked to venture etc.

The revelations were deliciously innocent. One couple got together after a boy spotted her eating chips and decided to take one from her bag, leading them to munch the rest together – and go out for the following three months. Another met his girlfriend when he was knocked off his motorbike and found her at his side in the hospital, his assigned nurse. And in an example that proved personal ads still had their place, another young woman had simply answered an advert to a 'lonely sailor', along with five hundred others. He had picked her, 'and is now my fiancé'.

But as casual dating had taken hold of the teenage imagination, was marriage about to lose its allure? In 1958, the *Daily Mirror* reported on a University of California professor called Dr Kingsley Davis who claimed that early 'stupid-cupid' marriages made young people lazy and killed their spirit of rebellion.

A year later, *Daily Mirror* columnist Marjorie Proops reported on the phenomenon of the 'going steady' ring, a popularly exchanged gift in the US which was finally being produced in Blighty. The jewellers producing them in Britain, ever aware of British prudency, had even conceived of an economic loophole – if the 'going steady' led to engagement within six months, they would accept their return and put the credit – four pounds twenty shillings – to an engagement ring.

Between the marriage boom and the going steady ring, something significant had happened – the notion of dating for its own sake rather than as a means to an end amongst all echelons of society, not just the Bohemian and well-to-do, had been planted. The seeds of the Sexual Revolution had been sewn.

Chapter Ten

The Sixties: Sex and the Singles whirl

In 1963, two beautiful brunettes became the unwitting poster girls for the 'new morality', a polite way to express what was known as the 'sexual permissiveness' of the most revolutionary decade yet. The first was Elizabeth Taylor, whose affair with Richard Burton was deliberately 'revealed' as part of the publicity for the historical blockbuster *Cleopatra*. She'd been in trouble with the morality police before – in 1958 – when it was reported that she'd broken up the marriage of Eddie Fisher and Debbie Reynolds. But this time around her sexual avariciousness was deliberately exploited for the benefit of her new film. It worked. The film grossed more than $70 million at the box office and Taylor was catapulted to an unprecedented level of stardom

The second brunette was a young nightclub dancer and girl-about-town called Christine Keeler, whose affair with War Secretary John Profumo was exposed to similarly stratospheric consequences, not only because here was a story about illicit sex, but because Keeler's connection with Soviet spy Yevgeny Ivanov potentially threatened national security.

For Britain at large, the most important thing the Profumo affair revealed was that inter-class relationships were still heavily frowned upon. The issue of Profumo being married and thereby cheating on his wife with Keeler seemed to be less important than the fact a Harrow- and Oxford-educated son of a baron had hooked up with a young, beautiful working-class woman who sometimes worked as a prostitute and fraternised with West Indian men. It was Keeler's rapid social ascent that had startled the great and the good of Britain as much as her captivating looks.

In fact, a story like Keeler's could only have happened in London. If Britain today is a tale of two countries, there was even more striking a divide between the capital and everywhere else in the 1960s. From miniskirts to Bond girls, sex emanated from the cosmopolis and exported its frisky image, not just up and down the country, but around the world. By 1970, there were an estimated fifty serious communes in Britain, and free love, once the preserve of the Bloomsbury set, had been revived by a new Bohemian elite. But for the majority of people, finding a good girl or boy to date, mate with and make a Formica and lino-decorated home with was still paramount.

In a BBC programme on the topic of marriage, broadcast in 1964, a group of senior school children were asked for their opinions on why they might wait to have sex until marriage. 'Respecting the girl' was the top answer, and the one best received by the interrogating teacher. When a National Opinion Poll, conducted in 1969, asked the same question, a geographical divide became apparent, with 70 per cent of people in Scotland thinking sex before marriage was wrong, a number which fell to 47 per cent in Wales and the West, 44 per cent in the North England, and a lowly 29 per cent in London and the South. Life in the South was simply sexier.

Nevertheless, there was a contradiction between what men and women said was the right thing to do and what they were actually doing. By the time the first Brook sexual health clinic opened in 1964, an estimated 480,000 women in Britain were already taking the oral contraceptive pill and, by 1969, 48 per cent of women under the age of twenty-three had taken it. Initially the Pill was available on the NHS to married women whose health was at risk in the case of further pregnancies. But in 1967, the National Health Service Family Planning Act recommended that contraceptive advice and supplies be given to all women in England and Wales. Family Planning in Britain was given the royal seal of approval in 1969 when the Duke of Edinburgh opened the Margaret Pyke Centre at the headquarters of the FPA. Roman Catholics naturally maintained opposition, but the majority of the country was coming to terms with contraception as a basic human right.

All this prevention of pregnancy might have been good for people's sexual freedom, but was it encouraging younger teens to become sexually active earlier? That was the worrisome question on everyone's minds. In a *Guardian* report from 1962, the marriage guidance counsellor Dr Wendy Greengross said that over the past decade, the age at which first courtship started had steadily dropped. 'We are now faced with this thing called "going steady" when boys and girls of 12 or 13 have an exclusive relationship with each other instead of going about in groups.'

Greengross went on to explain how this was a pattern they took on to their engagement, dating for a couple of years first, and offered a controversial view: that young teens were decidedly sexual, that their sexual powers 'declined' after the age of fifteen or sixteen. 'Immorality and heavy petting are due to ignorance. Most girls of 13 to 15 think that boys are merely girls in trousers and that their sexual reactions are just the same. They have no idea how sexually active their boy friends are. If girls realised these things fewer of them would get into trouble.'

However, Michael Schofield's book, *The Sexual Behaviour of Young People*, published 1965, proved quite the opposite. According to Schofield's research, kissing on a first date – of the chaste, closed-lip variety, rather than the French kind – was usually both men and women's first heterosexual contact.

Kissing was followed by eight different kinds of petting activities. Penetrative sex was certainly not inevitable, but when sex did occur, men said it was dependent on desire, women on feelings of love, and an overwhelming majority cited curiosity. Sex was still happening relatively late on. By the age of fifteen only about one in twenty boys and one in fifty girls went all the way.

Twelve was found to be the average age at which people found out about sex, with two-thirds of boys and a third of girls hearing nothing from their parents at all. Curiously, middle-class girls 'found out' about sex at the youngest age. Half of those surveyed who were sexually active both knew about and were using contraception, with a quarter saying they never did and a third of boys saying they 'didn't care' about it, an interesting turn up for the books, given that just thirty years earlier contraception had been a male responsibility.

As such, 'getting into trouble', despite the availability of contraception, was still happening on a fairly regular basis. In the early 1960s, one in every five brides was pregnant on their wedding day, and the *Daily Telegraph* estimated there were as many as fifty thousand illegal abortions being carried out every year. The majority of those surveyed were family-oriented and seeking marriage with kids, although a quarter wanted to have a 'good time' beforehand. The boys also confessed to wanting sex, but being morally critical of their female partners for letting them have it.

Still, whether you were going to get yourself into trouble or just have a whole lot of protected fun, there was still the matter of how you went about finding someone to do any of it with. In the 1960s, the dance hall had been superseded by the youth club as the best place to pick up a partner. In 1963, the National Association of Youth Clubs announced that its membership was up by 16,000, at an all-time high of 204,785 members, and that youth hostelling had also seen a massive expansion. Younger teens, meanwhile, aged twelve to fifteen, tended to frequent cafés, ice-cream parlours, parks and chip shops, which usually had a reputation amongst adults as being for 'lay-abouts'. This in turn only created a sense of rebellion and more of a 'pull' towards these places. Girls were usually expected to be in earlier, however, and drinking was frowned upon in case it put them in a compromising position.

Taking your date home was an important ritual. Either it was an opportunity for some furtive snogging, preferably behind a privet hedge or in the outhouse (many homes still didn't yet have an inside toilet), or a chance to prove one's decency to your girlfriend's parents. And it was clearly important. In the late 1960s, 47 per cent of boys and 34 per cent of girls had met the parents of the person they ended up marrying by the end of the first week in which they'd started going out.

For everyday couples moving towards marriage, rituals that had first taken off in Victorian times remained vital to doing romance right. Engagement rings were ever important, even if it was only a ring from Woolworths. In 1968, the average couple in Swansea spent £30 on an engagement ring, the equivalent of £492 today. What's more, being engaged without a ring was deemed to be slightly shameful, an indication that the man who'd proposed perhaps wasn't quite so interested in the lady in question after all. After the ring came the newspaper announcement, and then the all-important engagement party.

Parents who opposed their children's choice of partners could kick off but didn't have a legal leg to stand on. In the case of a young couple from Swansea called John and Jennifer, they even found themselves at a magistrates' court after Jennifer's father refused John's request for his daughter's hand in marriage. The situation was complicated when Jennifer found herself pregnant. As Jennifer recounted, 'My solicitor said my father objected because John was a labourer. He asked him "Do you have any labourers?" and my father said "Yes, and I think the world of them." "Why then do you object to your daughter marrying a labourer?" He couldn't say nothing then.'

The magistrate's conclusion was that the parents were in the wrong. The couple went to the register office that afternoon and got a licence to be married the following week.

As the music industry grew, and disposable income rose, how you defined yourself socially became ever important.

Mods were primarily working-class teenagers who lived mainly in London and the new towns of the South, and identified themselves by their sharp, minimalist clothing and rhythm and blues music taste.

They aligned themselves with the Italian Mafiosi and spent an unlikely proportion of their time 'being blocked', otherwise known as being high on amphetamines, besides riding around on their scooters and drinking cappuccino in the growing number of Italian café bars.

Mod life revolved around club life. In a *Sunday Times* article of 1964, the seventeen-year-old Denzil was interviewed describing his ideal week. Besides shopping for clothes and records on Saturday afternoon, dancing featured every night of the week, apart from Thursday 'reserved for the ritual washing of the hair'.

The Mod's rivals, Rockers, meanwhile, favoured leather jackets and faded blue jeans, long hair for the boys, lacquered and piled up high for the girls. Marijuana was their drug of choice, and sex a more openly favoured pastime.

In an interview with a young mod called Terry, published in the *Daily Express* in 1964, Terry carefully set out the differences between the two groups, in dress, in demeanour and in their propensity to fight. She also explained the fear Mod girls had over taking amphetamines: 'I have never taken any. I'm frightened to. They say girls who take them won't be able to have any babies and they harm your body.'

Both the interviews came as a result of a series of infamous clashes over Whitsun weekend in May 1964 at the seaside towns of Margate, Broadstairs and Brighton, when thousands of mods and rockers found themselves unwittingly at the same resorts and fought openly on the seafront. The groups had been labelled a national threat and the question of what to do about them was debated in Parliament.

Dating a boy on a bike brought with it the prospect of the 'ton-up' – a weekend away at the seaside, as part of a group of other young men and women doing the same. The group, to some extent, dictated the relationship. If the rest of the group didn't like you, it was all too easy to find yourself rejected by the boy you thought was your beloved.

Mod girls had a new kind of freedom. They didn't need to be coupled up to be accepted as part of the gang, and compared with Hell's Angels, mod boys didn't view them as accessories. In part, this was to do with the relative effeminacy of male mods – their preoccupation with their style and looks – but it was also a sign of the times. Earning their own money and being able to take charge of their reproductive future was enabling women to carve out stronger identities for themselves.

But whatever new sexual arrangements were now on the table, the fierce tribalism of the two groups meant love between a mod and a rocker was strictly socially prohibited. There aren't even any *Romeo and Juliet*-style news reports from the period.

Alongside Mods and Rockers, if there's one thing we associate with the 1960s, it's the miniskirt. When a young British fashion designer called Mary Quant invented it, she couldn't have known the insalubrious impact six inches above the knee was about to have on the moral fabric of society.

But the miniskirt turned out to be more than a metaphor for the permissive society. Instead, it had a tangible impact on day-to-day dating behaviours.

Most men had simply never seen that much flesh on display on a day-to-day basis, and as much as inviting the idea of more sex, it created all kinds of debate about whether it was wise to 'go with' a girl that wore one.

In 1966, the Spanish police fined miniskirted girls holidaying in Costa Brava for offences against public morality and miniskirts could even start family rows. A court report from the *Daily Telegraph* in 1967 recounted a tale about how one 'Kathleen Brookman, 17, a tall brunette, shortened her mini-skirt by 3 inches', only to invite a reprimand from her father. When her mother intervened, he ended up striking her, which led to the female recorder hearing the case to pronounce: 'It's a great pity this should happen to a family like yours [. . .] It might be a good thing, however, to have a husband who does care about his daughter's appearance.' As a result of the disturbance, Kathleen left home.

Miniskirts were even blamed for declining sales of mistletoe, according to a Covent Garden buying agent called Cecil Dixon: 'It's a fast disappearing thing now people have sex all the year round. The miniskirt is pushing mistletoe out.'

Women in the sticks took a more cautious approach, stitching matching knickers to sit under their own homemade skirts and protect their modesty. Then in 1966, the *Daily Mail* carried a story about sixteen-year-old trainee bricklayer Tony Liggard of King's Lynn who had opted to don a fourteen-inch little purple number for a shopping trip with his trouser-clad female companion, the male miniskirt's designer, Toni Byrne. Although Byrne said she wouldn't recommend it for men with really hairy legs, Liggard concluded that it was 'no more feminine than shoulder-length hair' and had no doubt the fashion would catch on. It didn't, but that nod to male sartorial experimentation hinted at a trend that was yet to come.

At the end of the 1950s, young women were still getting most of their relationship advice from magazines, most of which gave relatively conservative-minded recommendations. But in the early 1960s this changed with the launch of three magazines – *Honey*, *Jackie* and *Fabulous* – and the publication of American editor Helen Gurley Brown's *Sex and the Single Girl*. First published in the US, the book was an instant best-seller on both sides of the Atlantic, mainly because Brown's recommendations weren't about apologising for female sexuality ('perhaps you will reconsider the idea that sex without marriage is dirty'), nor about finding a way to merely tolerate singledom as *How To Live Alone and Like It* had done some thirty years before. Instead, *Sex and the Single Girl* assured its readers that economic and spiritual independence were prerequisites for attracting the best kind of partner, and that the book itself wasn't about 'how to get married but how to stay single – in superlative style'. Sex was a liberal bounty, while cooking well for yourself, maintaining your own apartment, 'even if it's over a garage', and not harbouring 'an ounce of baby fat' were the ways to ensure you a singlehood in which you could revel.

Then in 1965, the publishing company George Newnes launched *Nova*, a women's magazine intended to reach the educated women's market, written for and by women of a 'progressive' persuasion, who had faith in sex reform, reproductive rights, and positioned themselves against racism, sexism and poverty. Its audience was perceived as feminists in an era when feminists were still seen by the general populace as aggrieved spinsters or agitating bluestockings. These readers were turning their backs on the notion that women enter marriage as virgins, that women were responsible for the success of their marriages, and that divorce was not an option for anyone but the supremely well-to-do and well connected (prior to the reform of the divorce laws in 1969, long-term adulterous liaisons were still preferable to the social shame that came of being divorced).

As such, the magazine started to write about sex and dating in a way that better reflected the relationships people were actually having, rather than just those they were prepared to admit to. Between its quixotically designed pages, women admitted to never having loved their husbands, but having married them to satisfy their parents. Wives and mistresses were interviewed side by side (though anonymously for their own protection), putting forward a double-pronged 'other woman' perspective.

Male confessions were included too. A doctor called Brian Inglis wrote a piece for the magazine questioning why having sex with a patient was such a terrible idea, while a poet called Dom Moraes confessed to struggling to reconcile his animal and romantic sides and the way he would classify women according to which emotion they provoked in him.

Not that men didn't have their own publications in which to ruminate over such conundrums. It sounds like a joke today, but *Playboy* really was a revolutionary publication when it first graced shelves in 1953, featuring Marilyn Monroe skimpily clad on the cover and unabashedly nude inside. Pin-up photography was not new. As early as 1935, Britain had its own 'girlie' mag, *Men Only*, and then

Lilliput, launched in 1937. What was new was a magazine aimed specifically at men, designed not to dictate what you couldn't do sexually, but to celebrate what you could – even if that celebration was somewhat in favour of getting it on with gorgeously proportioned women.

In many ways Hugh Hefner used himself as the model for the aspirational male he wished to celebrate. Having written his university thesis on Kinsey, on graduating he'd worked as a struggling copywriter and sometime cartoonist, soon married with a young child. But within a decade of the magazine's launch, he had transformed himself into a bon vivant bachelor, lacking in neither beautiful women, nor a bevy of consumerist goods.

There was nothing here about having to kill bears or fight for one's country (Hefner, notably, had done national service). Instead, how to pick everything from the perfect martini to the perfect shade of shirt filled its pages, alongside in-depth enquiries into sexual trends. Hefner invented the metrosexual before he was ever a twinkle between David Beckham's sarong-clad thighs. When the magazine was launched in Britain in the early 1960s, it soon achieved a circulation of ninety thousand, and it paved the way for the launch of Bob Guccione's *Penthouse* in 1965. Even Gloria Steinem is once said to have admitted that *Playboy* was partly responsible for the sexual revolution.

But the sexual revolution didn't strike everyone as beneficial. Feminists of the era saw it as a male opportunity to exploit women for their own sexual gains. Free love was a ruse; it meant men could now have all the sex they liked without ever having to commit to the woman that was giving it to them.

Relationships depicted in London amongst the creative and musical elite only added to the allure. Take tales of the Rolling Stones and their various partner-swapping escapades which formed tabloid fodder for decades even after their heyday. Marianne Faithfull, the then girlfriend of Mick Jagger, would say she would go on to spend a night with bandmate Keith Richards only because she was following Mick's orders.

Speaking in the 1970s in the *NME* about their relationship, she recalled how unhappy he made her and the jealousy she felt when she realised he was basically able to channel her anguish into brilliant song-writing. Her conclusion? 'I don't like [men] them very much. They're there to be used. I know that's not true but it's how I was brought up to think.'

Faithfull would later go on record as saying that she only managed to have sex with the help of drink or drugs. But for many women, it was a more pleasant experience. Andrea Adam, a reporter for *Time* magazine felt positively about her own sexual experimentation: 'It was part of my growth as a human being, as a woman and as a feminist . . . I wanted women to become equal and I wanted permissiveness.'

Meanwhile, men were just as likely to experience inner discord. An anonymous source interviewed by author Cate Haste in her book, *Rules of Desire*, noted, 'We had been brought up traditionally, even strictly, and to try to leap out of your own habits and upbringing into this blissful state where there were no hang-ups was of course interesting psychologically but it was completely impossible.'

But for Rosie Boycott, the founder and editor of the feminist magazine *Spare Rib*, 'there was still a power game going on in that women were typists, men were the bosses, men were the ones who decided what wages people got, whether people had jobs. Women were dependent on men.'

But both women and gay men were about to experience the greatest sexual freedom they had to date. New sex research from the American duo Masters and Johnson published in 1966 was exploding various myths about female sexuality, and their findings were even more radical than those of Kinsey, such as distinguishing between the clitoral and the vaginal orgasm.

Then, in 1968, the Sexual Offences Act, which decriminalised homosexual acts between consenting adults in private and had been introduced as a result of the Wolfenden inquiry was finally passed. It still had limitations – it excluded the armed forces, and the age of consent remained at twenty-one for homosexuals, compared with sixteen for heterosexuals, but gay men could finally have gay sex in the privacy in their own homes without fear of reprimand. Dating, however, would take another decade.

Meanwhile, interracial marriage was becoming ever common; even if mixed-race couples still faced open and vocal prejudice on the streets, high-class white women and working-class black men mingled and drank together in the same smart London clubs, while the first interracial kiss was shown on television, featured in an episode of the popular soap *Emergency Ward 10*.

High-profile interracial couples – Mick and Bianca Jagger, Michael and Shakira Caine, John and Yoko Lennon – also made it more acceptable, even fashionable, to date outside of one's own race. And when the cover of Jimi Hendrix's third studio album, *Electric Ladyland*, was released in 1968, it generated a plethora of sales and acclaim, as well as a modicum of controversy, by featuring a bevy of naked female beauties of all races luxuriating alongside one another.

The 1960s was also the decade in which kinky sex started to become, if not more socially acceptable, certainly more readily available. Throughout the 1960s, two men, Edward Donelly and James McGuigan, were the editors and printers of two magazines called *Exit* and *Way Out*. Each edition featured around three hundred ads, each offering various kinds of sexual experimentation. Each private ad featuring a minimum of twenty-four words cost just £1 to place, and everyone from the straight to the gay to the transgender, interested in everything from whipping to restraining to wife-swapping, dared to reach out for the like-minded.

That they featured adverts from gay men and women didn't trouble Donelly and McGuigan – homosexuality was, after all, legal. But publications could still be prosecuted under the charge of corrupting public morals and, in due course, *Exit* and *Way Out* were considered to have done exactly that. When the police came to seize the incriminating material, they noted the names and addresses of more than four hundred advertisers and set to paying them each a visit. As per police suspicions, many of those interviewed, it turned out, were prostitutes using the magazine's pages to court clients. It would be just one example of how alternative sexualities, paid or otherwise, were persecuted together.

Still, that didn't stop the decade from resisting the import of swinging from the US. With its roots in the 1920s exploration of alternative lifestyles, the Americans took to swinging as they had to swing-dancing. In 1959, the extent of couples swapping partners at private parties in America was revealed by a Stateside publication called *Mr*, which conducted an intimate reader survey before publishing the lascivious results. From Chicago to San Francisco, far more Americans, it turned out, enjoyed open sex outside of their marriages than had ever been anticipated. By 1961, discreet ads for swingers had started to crop up in mainstream publications such as the *San Francisco Chronicle*, apparently placed by something called the Sexual Freedom League. In Britain, *Exit* and *Way Out* carried the same. Eustace Chasser, a Scottish doctor specialising in sexuality and the author of many books on the topic, was one of the first open advocates of swinging, believing, along Freudian lines, that the freedom it afforded resulted in a more relaxed relationship with sexual desires. Eventually, the police's interest in such ads in *Exit* and *Way Out* waned and, by 1971, *Time Out* was carrying open invitations to swing.

But if personal ads had become the preserver of sexual risk-takers, there was a newer, more hi-tech way of meeting on the horizon. In 1959, two Stanford engineering students designed a class project called Operation Match, which used the IBM 7090 to match up a pool of forty-nine men and forty-nine women. After filling in a paper questionnaire, which they mailed into the group along with $3, the answers were punched into the computer, before each individual received a printout of the matches' names and phone numbers. By the autumn of 1965, six months after its launch, ninety thousand Operation Match questionnaires had been completed, making the founders $270,000 in profit ($1.8 billion in today's money). 'We supply everything but the spark,' chimed its co-founder Jeffrey Tarr.

It would be a few more years before the English equivalent was launched. In the meantime, Brits would be left to their own spark-inducing devices. The lights were about to go off – and on.

Chapter Eleven

The Seventies: The Joy of Vexing Mary Whitehouse

In 1970, an unmarried couple could still not book a double room at Claridge's yet this was also the year the first photograph of a topless model, Stephanie Rahn, appeared in a mainstream newspaper – the *Sun* – and that Germaine Greer published her seminal work, *The Female Eunuch*. Far from paving the revolutionary road, what the 1960s had merely done was to prepare a ready-to-unravel carpet.

For teenage girls, the publication shaping their worlds was *Jackie*. First published in 1964, it wasn't until the 1970s that it became a real cultural tour de force. At the height of its circulation in 1976, it was selling more than half a million copies an issue and it was by far the most influential source of information on love, sex and relationships available to its young female readers.

Jackie wasn't radical; it focused on pleasing boys, entertaining its readers' teeny-bopper fantasies about the most toothsome celebrities, instructing readers how to flatter their figures, and giving them a smattering of other love and career advice. But its chatty tone created a ludicrously loyal readership. At a time when sex education in schools was still scant, it gave a much-needed sisterly steer.

What's more, it never patronised its readers, taking their adolescent relationships seriously, and encouraging girls to be as autonomous in their own lives as they could muster.

In an article on 'problem boys', entitled 'What Makes You Love Them?', the opening para stated, 'It's just a fact of human nature that we tend to fall for the rotten boys. We have this romantic idea that men should be tough and dominating and most girls are automatically attracted to the worst ones out!'

So Jackie very helpfully listed the most difficult six types, which included:

The Hard type – with a soft centre!
The Unobtainable type
The Unromantic type
The Lady Killer
The Possessive Domineering type
The Plain Rotten type

Cathy and Claire were the magazine's resident agony aunts, attracting more than four hundred letters a week, and answering questions on everything from body hair to pregnancy scares.

In a letter entitled, 'I'm scared to kiss him!!', an anxious reader lamented how she couldn't bring herself to touch lips with Geoffrey: 'I've known him all my life and don't really like him that much. I never let him kiss me. Whenever he tried I would turn away . . . now I've been asked out by Keith and I just have to go, because I've fancied him for ages. The trouble is I just don't know what to do. I'm so worried.'

The reply concentrated on relaxing the girl in question – 'Everyone has to have a first time, including Keith! It's our guess that he'll be just as nervous as you – not because he's never kissed anyone before, but because he's never kissed YOU before.'

In another feature, 'Are You the Girl for Him?', Donny Osmond, Bryan Ferry, the Bay City Rollers and David Essex were each asked what they liked women to wear. While both David Essex and Brian Ferry agreed that 'ugly platforms' were seriously inelegant, some of the further quotes are detailed to the point of parody. Would David Essex really have said, 'As for materials, my favourites are crepe and beautiful old prints'? The Bay City Rollers, meanwhile, had kept it simple by expressing a preference for girls dressed in 'rollers' fashions' – simple jeans and t-shirts – although 'girls should still look like girls so we think long hair helps'.

But as radical feminist *Spare Rib* magazine pointed out, publications such as *Jackie* often created the problems it sought to solve. *Spare Rib*, meanwhile, was more akin to a publication shared by the Suffragettes. Articles included features on what it was like be pregnant and no longer the object of the male gaze – essentially, on how men stopped hitting on you accordingly once they viewed you as 'another man's property'; how disabled women had sex, and how lesbians thought about how they'd become lesbian. Here was a bolder way to look at sex, relationships and consciousness that may or may not filter out to the masses. But for the women that did come upon it, it was consciousness raising of the highest level.

It was joined by *Forum* magazine, 'the journal of human relations'. Started in 1965, *Forum* was a seriously intelligent take on sexuality with a political bent – it wanted to properly educate its readers about every biological and psychological component of sex. In the early 1970s its subscription ran into the tens of thousands, although it was delivered to most people's postboxes via brown paper envelope post. Besides offering scientifically sound assessments of impotence, group sex and the risk of thrombosis from the Pill, for example, it also investigated whether hypnotic suggestion could increase bust size. Anal sex, pornography as therapy and brothels for women were all investigated.

Its female journalists wrote candidly and confessionally: 'Eventually I found that making love as an emancipated woman doesn't really consist of jumping in and out of bed with anyone who is available and sends out a few signals,' confessed one Phyllis Raeder, while an essay on work-sharing by Sandra McDermott proposed that men and women share a job and childcare, thus unburdening both of them. By 1974, *Forum* was openly carrying gay love-making tips, and it almost obsessively celebrated the female orgasm.

But it was Forum's readers' letters that offer the most cogent insight into what men and women in the early 1970s were getting up to, even although admittedly many of the letters came from those who claimed to be already married, but in reality were not necessarily hitched.

Take this one entitled 'The Smell of Fish': 'As one who is highly sexed, I am also stimulated greatly by the sight and smell of wet fish.' It then goes on to relate the tale of how this fetish came from him being an errand boy for a fishmonger and his wife, who one day caught him masturbating whereupon she made him give her oral sex. 'There was a delightfully warm fishy smell in the shop which was analogous to the odour of her genitals.'

There was another amusingly confessional letter from a member of a 'bell circle' – a group of men who attached cat-collar bells to their penises: 'Our most recent achievement occurred last week in the men's lavatory at Victoria Station when the eight of us, before adjusting our dress, played "Bells Across the Water" much to the enjoyment, if not edification, of many onlookers . . . I would mention that we are available at a small charge for parties, picnics and, of course, balls.'

Forum's editor's reply? 'Don't ring us – we'll ring you!'

But when it came to widespread cultural influence, magazines didn't stand a chance against the growing ubiquity of TV. And if *Forum* magazine was the nation's dirty cerebral uncle, then *Top of the Pops* was its glitzy, exhibitionist niece.

When Mark Bolan first appeared on the music show wearing glitter, he spawned more or less instant imitation. They might have shunned the velvet and skintight satin for workaday flares and plaid shirts, but soon young working men everywhere from Glasgow to Gateshead were rocking shoulder-length locks – with a hairnet atop if need be for safety at work. When David Bowie announced in an interview given to *Melody Maker* in 1972, that he was, if not gay, at least bisexual, it was a fairly radical confession, especially given that homosexual sex had only been declared legal some five years before.

After all, in the early 1970s it was still common for pubs to reject gay couples for holding hands, and for gay men and women to be assaulted on the street. Police officers in plain clothes were even used for entrapment, sent into pubs as a deliberate 'lure', able to make an arrest if they were approached by anyone looking for sex. In response, a tiny coalition of determined protestors established the Gay Liberation Front to challenge such practises. In 1972, a summer protest in London's Hyde Park, involving a teen Peter Tatchell, would become known as the UK's first Gay Pride March. By 1974,the GLF had splintered and become half a dozen campaign groups, laying the ground for larger organisations including Stonewall and Outrage! But in its four short years, it made a significant social impact, spreading the word at colleges and universities that it was OK to want a same-sex relationship, giving advice about how to conduct one's life as a gay man or woman at a time when society was only just beginning to accept that gay relationships were acceptable.

But while bisexual experimentation might have been fashionable for pop stars such as Mick Jagger and David Bowie, most people weren't any more adventurous. As Michael Des Barres, a 1970s artist and actor recalls, 'there was a very specific bunch of guys who were androgynous, and who were into that debauchery, but – and this is where a lot of people miss the point – they weren't gay. A lot of people talking and writing about this period focus on boys fucking boys, when in fact it was boys who looked like girls fucking girls.'

As it turned out, amongst the musical elite, it was also boys fucking girls who looked like they still regularly wore a school uniform.

The year 1970 saw the release of the film *Groupie Girl*, in which a lissom twenty-year-old named Sally works her way around, up and under a band named 'Opal Butterfly' whom she hops on tour with. It was a fictional drama, but inspired by the heart-stopping groupie scene that was in full swing by the 1970s.

Interestingly the film's director, Ashley Kozac, who had previously managed American folk-pop star Donovan, described his creation as a film that would showcase 'the sick minds' of the groupies, while 'deter many young teenagers' from becoming them. It's hard to know if he was right. It certainly did nothing to assuage the original scene on the other side of the Atlantic, where even younger girls, nicknamed 'baby groupies', slept with rockers including Jimmy Page, Iggy Pop, David Bowie and the Stones.

In fact, by 1973, there was even a publication dedicated to helping them share tips (although how to beat off the competition was a component part of that), in the form of the cult US groupie fanzine *Star*. So controversial did it turn out to be that it only lasted five issues. But those five issues offer a lip-smacking insight into the supposed mindset of a rock-cock-hungry teenage girl.

Articles such as 'Can You Be Satisfied With Only One Guy?', and 'How to Do Anything You Want and Get Away With It' give you a flavour of the rebellious philosophy on offer. This magazine wasn't just about bypassing the statutory rape law in order to bag a rock god between your barely shaved thighs. It was about how to break the rules of conventional sexuality, where timorous, meek women awaited men's meaty advances.

Star was well aware of its provocative powers. The letters page, full of real or fake correspondence from outraged parents, affronted competing males and disgusted nun-teachers were met with suitably desultory replies. The language and tone often sounded fictional.

Take this from one Eileen Funkhouser:

Dear *Star*

Your magazine is so trashy. I wouldn't even use it for the bottom of my birdcage. Who do you think you are? Girls could get pregnant or VD just following your advice.

The reply?

Dear Eileen

You can hate *Star* but why be so uptight and try to run other people's lives? We hope that printing your letter will show you that we let everyone do their own thing, whether they agree with you or not.

When the ideas in Germaine Greer's *The Female Eunuch* began to percolate through society, it became common currency for women to expect to sleep with multiple sexual partners without any real attachment. There was a notion that if you weren't doing so, you weren't really fully embracing your sexuality. As an 18-year-old commune dweller called K. A. Silverstone recalls, 'having indiscriminate sex was one of the ways of rejecting societal norms. Our parents were still stuck with the idea of sex outside of marriage as being something shameful and dirty'.

But for many women, it simply didn't feel that satisfying, and despite the availability of contraception, virginity was still a highly prized commodity. As a teenager of the time called Chris Arthur recalls, 'Without going into the gory details, my girlfriend would let me do practically anything I wanted, as long as it did not involve actual intercourse. She was determined to save herself for marriage . . . There was a superstitious regard for virginity, which was defined in a very narrow sense.'

Meanwhile, 1970s wife-swapping parties, while the stuff of legend, seemed to have a factual precedent. In 1969, the Liberal candidate for Basildon, Essex, Stanley Balls, alleged in Parliament that the town's housewives were so bored and depressed that they were turning to wife-swapping parties for respite. The problem, a local vicar and GP suggested was because Basildon was a new town where young marrieds without family ties struggled to feel connected to the community. Although nobody interviewed at the time seemed to want to admit to knowing anything about it, a group of local women soon took matters into their own hands by starting up an anti-boredom group designed as an antidote to the lascivious problem.

But fear of wife-swapping escalated. In 1972, a 31-year-old man called Vincent Williams from Reading was jailed after petrol-bombing the caravan of Quentin and Gwendoline Hind, the couple he and his wife Christine had played with. The wives had apparently formed a lesbian relationship after being shown pornography by Hind, which led the judge to conclude 'there was a deliberate attempt to corrupt by pornography. It would be interesting if those who believe pornography does not corrupt were shown the papers in this case. It certainly did here.' Who knew petrol-bombing could be so readily identified as a consequence of porn consumption?

But were couples safer off at home?

From *The Sweeney* to *Bouquet of Barbed Wire*, in the 1970s television made even the most conservative home a porthole to a world of free love, homosexual affairs, endemic infidelity and physical pleasures many Brits may not have stumbled upon otherwise. Take the Roman period drama *I, Claudius*. Up to twenty million viewers at a time were drawn into the complex and lascivious plots featuring imperial orgies, fucking competitions and incest. Nudity had been almost completely taboo on TV during the 1950s and '60s, but now you didn't need to hunt out explicit display, just turn on the TV after 9 p.m. (the watershed had been introduced as part of the 1964 Television Act).

Meanwhile, explicit magazines and books were easier to come by than ever. A relaxation of obscenity laws meant that men's glossies such as *Men Only*, *Mayfair* and *Penthouse* were racking up sales of more than one and a half million each. Add in the national strikes, power cuts, financial instability and the introduction of alcohol for sale at home, and staying in offered most a better date night option.

On the other hand, while drama got a titillating pass, any serious examination of sex was still considered taboo. In 1976, Thames TV pulled a series called *Sex In Our Time*, a seven-part, seven-hour investigation into British habits, which looked at everything from secret same-sex relationships to couples in sex therapy and took more than a year to make. The one sequence that troubled head honchos in particular was a segment showing a women's group using a spectroscope to examine their own cervixes and before the show was due for transmission, they balked and pulled the whole series.

Then, in 1978, the Family Planning Association complained that it was not allowed to promote responsible contraceptive use, while drama and comedy could readily promote the opposite.

Such censoriousness wasn't built on mere speculative anxiety about complaints. As a new medium, television felt it couldn't afford undue negative publicity. After all, this was the decade of Mary Whitehouse, the former school teacher and one-woman complaints house, who made a second career for herself as the nation's moral censor. Along with her friend, Norah Buckland, a rector's wife, Whitehouse had produced a manifesto to battle against lasciviousness on TV: 'We call upon the BBC for a radical change of policy and demand programmes which build character instead of destroying it, which encourage and sustain faith in God and bring Him back to the heart of our family and national life.'

Whitehouse's objections weren't just restricted to the small screen, but to the radio too. She strongly objected to the Rolling Stones' album *Exile on Main Street* being played on BBC Radio 1 on the basis that it contained a four-letter expletive and, in 1977, began campaigning against the publication *Gay News*, claiming that its open celebration of homosexuality was blasphemous. Alarmingly, in the obscenity case that Mary Whitehouse brought, the jury sided with her and the magazine and its editor were forced to pay out fines of £1000 and £500 respectively. Inadvertently, the magazine's circulation actually went up as a result of the court case and it became evident that much of Britain was far gay-friendlier than Whitehouse and her acolytes would have liked to believe.

But the point remains that the reach television could have on everyday Britons meant that the conversations people were having about sex and relationships were changing.

Meanwhile, another kind of technology was incubating. In 1971, just three years after Operation Match had been developed in America, the *Observer* began to run ads from a company called 'Dateline', a British computer-dating company which promised potential clients a bank of some fifty thousand participants to choose from, 'more people than you could possibly get to know intimately if you spent a lifetime trying'. The Dateline system promised that it was the most sophisticated in Europe, running on a £65,000 IBM System 3 computer, with a questionnaire devised by computer experts and psychologists.

Dateline's founder, a former engineer called John Patterson, also created a magazine called *Singles*, and launched a travel agency, Singles Holidays, in 1975, both of which folded within a few years, but Dateline lasted right up until Patterson's death in 1998, whereupon it was sold to Columbus Publishing Group for nearly one and a half million pounds.

But users were cautious. In 1976, the Office of Fair Trading conducted an inquiry into computer dating based on the sheer number of complaints it had received from consumers new to the invention. In a line of of complaint which could easily come from today's dating app users, mainly, it seemed that there were anxieties about whether participants had lied on the initial questionnaire given to them by Dateline when they signed up. In particular, the category causing concern was the 'attractiveness' one. It seemed that too many men were displeased with what had been presented to them as 'attractive', leading a Dateline employee to question the disenchantment. The 'martini-type social life nurtured by the media' is partly to blame for raising such unreal expectations in men of mediocre attractiveness themselves, she commented. 'I sometimes want to ask them when they last looked in a mirror.'

National papers, meanwhile, maintained caution. They wouldn't stoop to advertising singles themselves, but did advertise the services of agencies that could. A *Daily Mail*

Classified Advertising page from 1978 advertised the services of the Anglia Friendship Bureau, Orion Introductions, Jean's marriage agency and even an organisation masquerading itself as a personal ad in language which was now clearly recognisable: 'Divorced, lonely, bored, need friends? You'll find hundreds in Leisure Times.'

But if 1970s couples could make it past the date stage, they still needed a hand when it came to getting down to it in the bedroom. Enter the quintessential sex manual, *The Joy of Sex*, which appeared in 1972. Written by Dr Alex Comfort, a medical doctor who had been educated at Cambridge University, the manual was ground-breaking, not only in its frankness of tone and use of graphic illustrations, but because it covered such taboo topics as swinging, bondage and group sex, as well as including some outlandish suggestions for original sexy times, including sex on a moving motorbike and sex on horseback.

But as the book began to sell in droves, the more conservative national papers poured scorn on it, overanxious about the effect it was having on the nation's bedroom behaviours. The *Daily Telegraph* saw it as 'pornography . . . distorting [people's] attitudes to sex to a crippling extent. Neurotic sexual preoccupations have reached the dimensions of a national perversion.' But it was countered by champions such as Jill Tweedie who praised its ability 'to make even the rudest Soho-type goings-on seem the sort of activities you might just get away with at a trendy vicar's tea party'.

Of course, escaping home altogether could provide a better backdrop to greater amorous adventures. If the 1960s saw the dawn of the European package holiday, the 1970s saw the inception of Club 18–30, the notorious singles

holidays which would come to embody everything conserv-
atives feared about the unmarried hordes. But when they
were first established in 1970 by the Horizon group, the
idea wasn't to promote casual, sangria-drenched sex so
much as to create a simple alternative to holidays without
families or children. It wasn't until a specific advertising
campaign promoted the notion that these holidays were a
great way to notch up sexual escapades in a sun-and cock-
tail-soaked combination that the package holiday's notorious image came to be born.

But by 1974, such holiday romances were of course
being warned against for their insalubrious moral consequences. Reported in the *Daily Mail*, the Reverend Frank
Beech, priest in charge of St Mary's Church in Nottingham,
warned 'Many young people pin their hopes on the annual
holiday producing, as if by magic, some new friendship or
romance out of which will blossom a more permanent relationship. It is a cautionary thought that at holiday time we
do not always see people as they really are.'

A *Sunday Times* reporter from the end of the decade
gives a flavour:

I spent one night on the beach until 4 a.m. waiting for
Chas to finish and let me get back to bed. But he did give
me 1,000 pesetas to amuse myself with. As for my other
room-mate, he was sick in the sink on the second day.
Too much sangria. Despite that, he managed five girls in
our seven nights there. And one girl, I found out, had
tackled an equivalent number of blokes.

Besides, holidays were crucial for providing couples
with privacy.

In the 1970s, young people, especially in the suburbs and from working-class backgrounds still lived at home until they got married. This made the notion of 'private time' pretty much impossible. And while the three-day week may have helped married couples have more sex, for those living under the auspices of their parents, it simply meant there were more people around to monitor you.

If the mean streets weren't your preferred hang out, youth clubs and dance halls were still the most popular venues for teens to meet. Dance halls and discos which doubled up as youth clubs were perfect, being adult venues that catered to teenage dreams. They played glam rock which was DJd and contained suitably high booths in which to hide and 'neck'. As ever, poorer young people simply did not have the resources to find designated, discreet indoor venues in which to be amorous. My mother recounts to me the glories of the privet hedge on the estate in West Yorkshire in which she grew up: 'At the end of the night, you could walk home to kiss behind it. My very tall privet hedge was the envy of my friends.'

Although many teenagers spent time at one another's houses, going up to someone's room was simply not done. Instead, a work-round was listening to music in the parlour – with the volume turned tactfully up.

Invariably, this practice of secrecy led to many a teen pregnancy. Teen abortions were at a rate of twenty thousand a year in 1971 and the attitude of the medical profession was that contraception was better than abortion. The Pill may have been synonymous with the swinging '60s but it wasn't until the 1970s that it began to have a widespread social impact. When Harold Wilson returned to office, he abolished prescription charges for birth control. Family

Planning Association clinics became part of the NHS, and by the end of the decade eight out of ten young women had taken the Pill, now the most popular form of contraception.

For a while, there was a disjunct in the law which meant it was legal to have sex at sixteen, but not to dispense contraceptives to under-eighteens without parental consent. In these cases, it was at the discretion of a specific GP to prescribe the Pill, which could cause chaos in a family practice if doctors disagreed with one another. But by the end of the decade the *Daily Mirror* was reporting on a group of men that were involved in an experiment to develop the male Pill, even if it was met with female cynicism: 'They know some men will say anything when they get that gleam in their eye.'

A survey of young women in their twenties on their opinions of teenage sex conducted by *Forum* magazine in 1974 is telling. Most of the girls offer contradictory, anxious opinions on what they think the right age is to lose one's virginity.

As the article concludes, 'the rapid decline of our morals is perhaps not such a foregone conclusion as many people would have us believe'.

But women were no longer waiting until their wedding nights to have sex, with three out of four who got married between 1971 and 1975 confessing to already having got frisky with their husbands before they walked up the aisle. When a researcher called Michael Schofield asked a group of 25-year-olds their opinions on premarital sex, only 4 per cent considered it wrong for an unmarried couple in love to get down to it.

Even if a sense of a woman on the Pill being 'easy' lingered in the minds of suburban curtain-twitchers, research from the time proved that it was those that shunned contraception that were the most sexually active. A survey of 2,995 women from 1971 who had unwanted pregnancies found that the more sexually active they were, the less likely they were to use contraceptives, and hardly any of the most sexually active used birth control at all. Similarly, in the 1970s there was a rise in VDs, not because people were having more sex, but because there was an anxiety about admitting you were having sex in the first place. This in turn prevented people from seeking treatment for symptoms, which led to more inadvertent spreading of disease.

But the conversation had changed. The year 1978 saw the first Women's Liberation Movement conference, and Erica Jong released her ground-breaking book, *Fear of Flying*, the tale of a doctor's wife who embarks on a rite of passage of infidelity and sexual self-discovery. Selling three million copies in its first year, it introduced the concept of 'the zipless fuck'– casual sex on a woman's terms – to a generation of women who now had the contraception with which to armour themselves. In the US, the Hite Report, surveying the sex lives of American women, concluded that orgasm was strong and easy for women, if they only received stimulation in the correct way.

So if women could plot their own careers, own their own homes and control their reproductive destiny, it's little wonder that by the end of the decade, divorce was at an all-time high. With some 129,000 cases being filed a year, the *Daily Mirror* conducted an investigation into the popularity of the new wave of marriage agencies that were taking full advantage of those statistics. Agencies such as the Katharine Allen bureau in Mayfair charged a £5 fee for an initial interview 'to put off customers out for a laugh', then charged £45 for registration, £45 for a year's introductions and £450 to ensure the dating process resulted in a walk up the aisle itself. By comparison, the bluntly named 'Needa Frend' based in Manchester charged £10 for life membership and £2.50 for lists of names every six months, catering in particular to women 'who can't get out and about the way men can', according to agency proprietor John McCormack.

Suddenly, the matchmakers were back in business. Yet the advice they were doling out could have been thirty years old. Women were advised to let the man pay, but avoid ordering items such as lobster or out-of-season strawberries, and, for both men and women, to avoid talking about anything more pertinent than the weather or other similarly neutral topics.

And as for sex on the first date? Men should remember that women had 'many good reasons for abstaining', but to avoid citing firm personal or religious principles as a reason for evading sex unless they were genuinely held convictions.

The advice was completely out of step with the cultural times. On the big screen, saucy films were raking in the viewers. From *Caligula*, which featured incest and sex with horses, and, at a cost of $17.5 million, would go down in history as the most expensive adult movie of all time, and *10*, a US comedy which launched the career of Bo Derek and introduced the world to the concept of 'the Perfect 10', the new sexual possibilities presented on screen were catering to the tastes of an ever-streetwise audience. Neither divorcees nor the women that had come of age in the 1970s could be repackaged as virgins, which was as much a victory owed to capitalism's filthy embrace as it was to women's rights.

But would Britain, now under the remit of a Conservative female Prime Minister, step up to claim the alternative, sexually liberated future it had plotted out for itself? Or would the old, enfettering triad of money, social status and blood lines continue to dictate the dating game?

Chapter Twelve

The Eighties: Aids and raves

The summer of 1981 was marked by riots and a royal wedding – THE Royal Wedding of the century, to be precise, between Prince Charles and Lady Diana Spencer. Twenty-eight million Britons, more than half the population, watched the extravaganza, with some 750 million more viewers around the world, more than the number that would go on to watch the nuptials between their son Prince William and Kate Middleton some thirty years later. Clearly money, social status and bloodlines continued to entertain public interest as much as any of the late 1970s new wave of soft porn films had. Royal subjects lined the bunting-festooned streets to wish them well, and most homes in the 1990s were still hoarding a mawkish souvenir from the gilded day.

The relationship would go on to generate endless column inches over the coming decades – column inches that would reveal the extraordinary details of the reality of their multiple tangled relationships with a whole cast of paramours and sycophants. PR was a burgeoning phenomenon, and not one the Royal Wedding family had yet come to grips with, which meant for a raft of incandescent personal revelations far more salacious than anything that hits today's Mail Online. Ranging from the story of Diana's bodyguard having been bumped off when she had an affair with him, to 'Tampongate', the infamous recorded private conversation between Charles and his lover Camilla Parker Bowles, theirs was the most talked-about relationship in 1980s media.

But at the time of the wedding, the narrative constructed was of a saccharine traditional fairy tale, with Charles making such platitudes as 'The glass slipper fitting sessions are over for me.'

Charles, of course, was hardly the nation's Prince Charming. That accolade went to Adam Ant, and his fellow New Romantics who had stolen the hearts of the nation's teenage girls by taking off from where the Glam Rockers of the 1970s had left. Also known as the Blitz kids, Futurists and New Dandies, their style was an idealised rebellion against the depression and unemployment that had begun to enmesh Britain, a more decadent and aspirational movement than punk which had straddled the span of the decades. Combining baggy trousers, spats, hats, brocade waistcoats and wide sashes, along with 1970s lace and velvet and make-up for both men and women, the movement was spawned out of a series of events at a venue called Billy's in Soho, the London version of New York's Studio 54, which vetted its entrants according to whether they were suitably glamorously attired. Soon, copycat club nights opened up across the country and sharing hairspray and eyeliner with your New Romantic partner was as integral a part of the relationship as sharing bodily fluids.

But even for those who were not so flamboyantly inclined, style and money were still a key part of the 1980s kiss-chase. Sales of cosmetics and clothes went through the roof as affordable high-street stores such as Next brought newfangled choice to male and female consumers.

Advertising was the new religion and images of hard-bodied, silk-skinned individuals with haughtily feathered haircuts the result of worshipping at that altar. The launch of MTV in 1981 created music video culture, which soon beamed bracing images of lissom-limbed models, yachts and souped-up cars situated in Bollinger-soaked resorts, all wrapped up in American veneers into British homes. Physical standards of beauty were at an all-time high. Yet at the same time economic uncertainty made hooking a life partner ever more desirable for those unable to climb the greasy capitalist pole. Gone was *The Joy of Sex*, in came titles such as *How to Make a Man Fall in Love With You*. Published in 1985, the book used the tricks of the sales industry to help women attract the right partner. Via 'The Man Plan', author Tracy Cabot helped readers to first identify what particular kind of prey they were stalking, before setting out the appropriate trap to help you ensnare his particular species. The book was a best-seller.

Dating had become a real commodification, and in the new free market, setting about making someone fall in love with you was just another point scored for the self-made man or woman.

Soon, Lonely Hearts adverts were riddled with the word 'solvent' – both men advertising it, and women requiring it. Writing in *Cosmopolitan* in 1987, Ian Collins observed that a man without means was a 'unisexual fantasy'. He went on, 'Many women are currently – as is usual in recession – being pushed into worse-paid jobs; and if women can't feed those charming little sprogs, the men will have to.'

If you really couldn't stomach dating a yuppie either, there was always the New Man. Derived from a term first coined in 1982 in a *Washington Post* article to describe

Dustin Hoffman's cross-dressing role in the film *Tootsie*, the New Man was proof that 1970s second-wave feminism had resonated somewhere along cultural lines.

In looks, he was paralleled in the entertainment world by androgynous celebrities such as Prince, Michael Jackson and the evergreen David Bowie. In personality, he cared about the environment, world poverty, and prioritised his partner's needs. He was no narcissist. He was in touch with his feelings and could readily express them. In a *Psychology Today* survey conducted in 1989, only thirteen women labelled him as 'sexy', with Jesus Christ labelled his number one role model. If ever a label was capable of a metaphysical castration, it was this. Even men embracing it were irate about it. 'Women go on and on about how they want us to be open and sensitive and bleed emotionally like they do,' said one respondent, 'then you take them at their word and open yourself up and have talks with them about your feelings and fears, and they turn on you.'

Equally, the new woman of the age did have something akin to her Edwardian namesake – only instead of votes and days out unchaperoned, she wanted unrivalled career opportunities by which she could make her own fortune. Welcome stage right, the Power-dressing Career Woman.

Flicking through magazines of the early 1980s, you could be forgiven for thinking women in their late twenties and thirties had almost boycotted men completely. Women were no longer being encouraged to consider at what point they might give up work upon marriage, or what part-time jobs might be compatible with raising a family and being a wife, but how they were going to grow their own nest egg. The 1980s *Cosmo* had no 'sex and relationships' section listed in its contents page, but a 'working woman' one. Articles with titles such as 'COULD You Live With Him?' and 'Mad About the Boys' about shelving marriage plans in exchange for teasing younger men were becoming the bedrock of the most popular glossies. Late 1970s feminism, combined with an economic crash and a self-serving female prime minister, was teaching women to find a relationship that prioritised their needs – or be prepared to go it alone.

Angling an older man, meanwhile, was to be avoided at all costs. As agony aunt Irma Kurtz had it: 'The average 43-year-old man is alone for a good reason. He may be a tidy, obsessional confirmed bachelor; he may have a secret affair going on with someone who is not free; he may be a homosexual; or he may simply not be interested.'

In 1984, the *Daily Mail* reported the results of a survey done by *Woman* magazine, all about relationships, accounting for six thousand single women, allegedly the largest study of its kind.

The survey proved that women were finding their feet as never before in relationships, and beginning to articulate what they really wanted, even if they were not yet always securing it for themselves. The results included the stats that nine out of ten women would like more cuddling and kissing before sex; that one in ten had enjoyed sex with another woman, and that the majority of women thought it was acceptable for both girls and boys to start having sex around the same age. Still, a surprisingly large three out of five of under nineteen-year-olds believed a couple should be in love or have plans to marry before they had sex. Eighty-five per cent who'd never been married still wanted to walk up the aisle. Forty-six per cent said both partners felt equally responsible for contraception, with around the same proportion saying they felt women were more responsible – a complete sea change to what had been stated by men in the 1930s. The Pill may have given women additional control, but it had also placed the burden of contraception squarely on their padded shoulders.

Still, at least the previous generation's obsession with being over the hill was waning. In a 1986 *Cosmopolitan* special on dating entitled 'Relax, It's Not the Royal Wedding', a feature was happy to proclaim, 'Fifteen years ago you were either married or dead at 35 . . . Now there are so many options available it's difficult to make one choice, one commitment.'

Here was the sea change; no longer a do-or-die economic necessity, you could now date for the sheer pleasure of it. Dating had become entertainment, and the entertainment industry had grasped that too. In 1985, ITV decided to launch a new-format Saturday night entertainment programme, presented by a former 1960s singer called Cilla Black. *Blind Date* was to become the template for British dating shows and magazine articles as we know them for the next thirty years. In its heyday, *Blind Date* attracted an audience of 18.2 million during its primetime Saturday-night slot, ran for eighteen series, and spawned the copycat shows *Take Me Out* and *The Love Machine* when its run came to an end in 2003. *Blind Date* even featured a number of minor TV celebrities as contestants, who attempted to use it as a launch pad for their entertainment careers, including presenter Amanda Holden, *Big Brother* contestant Nikki Grahame and comedian Ed Byrne. It even led to some lasting long-term relationships, including Alex and Sue Tatham, who went on to invite

Black to their wedding, and referred to her ever after as their 'fairy godmother'.

Obviously everyone didn't have a Cilla to hand. But there was another form of blind dating taking place, and that was via the pre-internet.

Bulletin board systems, known as BBSs, where committees could share messages with users plugged into a single modem became supremely popular in the 1980s and were the precursors to internet dating ads. Then in 1984, Matchmaker Network, the first online social network for marriage, was launched in the US. Comprising of a chain of fourteen BBSs, it covered Texas, California, Arizona, New York, Florida and Illinois. Users chose 'platonic' or 'romantic' mode and then shared and viewed messages accordingly, with non-members free to browse for three and a half hours, and then $50 for every hundred hours after.

In the early 1980s, some match-making agencies attempted to introduce video-dating to the singles market. The concept was pretty straightforward, with professional dating agencies taking professional videos of their clients which would then be available for other clients to view in their offices. Given that most of these individuals had no broadcasting experience, let alone practice in presenting themselves in the most interesting, suave and appealing way possible on camera, the results made for pretty uninspiring viewing. In fact, input 'video dating' into YouTube and you can see just how truly awkward the results turned out to be. They certainly make the Georgian gentlemen of eighteenth-century Lonely Hearts sound far more desirable, perhaps even exhumable, by comparison.

The most popular agency was called Great Expectations. At its peak the business had forty-nine franchises and made $65 million a year; not bad for a so-called dud of an idea. But although GE sold for $88 million dollars in 1995, the stigma of video-dating remained and it would be at least another decade before meeting online became something that slipped into easy public discussion. In fact, it took until the 1998 film, *You've Got Mail*, starring Megan Ryan and Tom Hanks was released, whereby the couple meet in an AOL chat room, for real-life couples to feel comfortable admitting just where in cyberspace they'd hooked up.

But there was one acronym that would be a dagger in the dating game; four small letters, a big disease with a little name, to quote Prince.

The history of Aids is a history of fear, bigotry and botched medical treatment, which began in America and infected the world. Back in 1981, the US Center of Disease Control reported that five young gay men had died from a rare form of pneumonia in Los Angeles. At the same time, St Mary's Hospital in London found immune cell abnormalities in blood samples from a hundred gay men, and, a year later, a 37-year-old called Terrence Higgins became the first known person to die of an Aids-related disease in London. It took until 1985 for the Department of Health and Social Security to set up an Aids Unit, and another year before Downing Street would issue a press statement, exhorting the general public to use condoms.

Looking after a dying partner became a feature of many gay men's lives.

But turning to a life of chaste monogamy was not on the cards for most. An attitude of a one-night stand being simply not worth it ransomed a few, but for the majority, HIV and Aids did not stem the amount of sex they were having, as was found by an organisation called Project Stigma. It found that, in a sample of 1083 men taken between 1987 and 1995, the majority of men in couples were in an open relationship and that there was actually an increase in anal sex, and oral anal sex – otherwise known as 'rimming' – because it was regarded as a low-risk HIV activity.

Press coverage of gay men and Aids in the 1980s was hugely unsympathetic. Here was the gay plague, a punishment of Old Testament proportions and the ultimate confirmation to the homophobes that they'd been right all along about the vagaries of the gay lifestyle.

Gay bashing, physical and verbal attacks, proliferated in Britain, (*Gay Times* estimated some fifty-five murders of gay men between 1986 and 1989) while Scotland Yard refused to monitor attacks on gay men until 1994, which had the effect of forcing LGBT dating underground once more. This was compounded by the fact the age of consent remained at twenty-one, meaning any men under this age were still liable for prosecution for indecency. The year 1989 saw 2022 prosecutions for indecency between men in England and Wales, the highest figure since 1955. You could also be prosecuted for breach of the peace if you were caught dressing in drag or kissing in public, and when it came to gay BDSM sexual activity, the precedent was set with Operation Spanner in 1990, a mass arrest in which gay men at a private play party were later prosecuted and jailed for up to four and a half years for indulging in BDSM practices amongst themselves. Public disapproval remained strong. According to the first NATSAL survey, more than two-thirds of men and more than half of women believed sex between two men to be nearly or always wrong, with only marginally less condemnation of it between two women.

With such a heavy focus on men, as activist and journalist Julie Bindel notes in her book, *Straight Expectations*, lesbians suffered from extreme marginalisation, often by gay males themselves, or had their children removed from them by social services. When the UK government introduced Section 28 into local authorities' educational policy, stipulating that schools should not 'intentionally promote homosexuality or publish material with the intention of promoting homosexuality', there was absolutely no reference made to women.

It makes sense that in the 1980s, Pride celebrations evolved as a way of bolstering connectivity and self-esteem amongst the gay community, as well as functioning as an ideal place to meet someone who might turn into a partner – whether that was for life, or the afternoon.

The Aids epidemic didn't just affect the gay community. By 1987, it was clear that the experimental sex that had been crucial to youthful rebellion and women finding a sexual identity of their own was over. Aids was viewed by a conservative morass as punishment for the decadence of previous generations.

As an article in a 1987 issue of *Cosmopolitan* pointed out, 'people who would once have been flirting away like civilised human beings are now channelling their energy into heated discussions of whether blood tests should be mandatory, and the pros and cons of having AIDS-free certificates to wave at prospective lovers'.

And it affected not just how people thought and taught about sex, but how they dated. In particular, the one-night stand, which had only just started to become a feature of every-day men's and women's lives in the 1970s, was out. By the end of the decade, some 62.5 per cent of women surveyed by NATSAL – the National Survey of Sexual Attitudes and Lifestyles – thought one-night stands wrong. Oral sex increased as a result of the anxiety over the risk of infection through penetration. And yet nearly a quarter of men and women were not using contraception at first intercourse compared with nearly 40 per cent back in the 1950s. Despite the advances made by the Pill, the condom had now become the first choice of contraception. What NATSAL also confirmed was that people were becoming sexually active earlier. The average man and woman who came of the age in the 1960s had lost their virginity at around age twenty. By the 1980s, this had dropped to seventeen. Young men and women of thirteen and fourteen were now reporting their first sexual experiences.

But it wasn't all amorous bounty. Somehow, inexplicably, the taboo about masturbation had crept back in, and questions about self-love were removed from the survey when it was discovered in the first draft that the participants – some sixteen thousand men and women aged between sixteen and fifty-nine – simply weren't willing to answer them.

One place everyone was having a lot of sex and not worrying in the slightest about the consequences, however, was in the decade's best-selling bonk-busters.

Authors such as Danielle Steele, Jackie Collins, Jilly Cooper and Shirley Conran, who penned 1982's best-selling *Lace*, made it their purview to dazzle a lust-lorn female readership with their tales of sex, sin, and mind-boggling social climbing set in glamorous locations where hard-bodied, moneyed and frequently aristocratic men seduced good girl after good girl.

But if Hollywood and Rio were locations never likely to harbour opportunity for the women of Bradford or Bognor Regis, soon, on the beaches of Mykonos, middle-aged women were to be found starring in their own amorous adventures. Inspired by Willy Russell's play, the film *Shirley Valentine* told the story of the eponymous Shirley, a Liverpudlian housewife who exchanges her evenings cooking egg and chips for her feckless husband Joe for those drinking local wine in the arms of Costas, a Greek taverna owner. It took a few years for the stories to filter through but soon the nationals were carrying tales of the real-life Shirleys – Suzy, a 42-year-old publisher from London who gave up her career to be with Zakynthian farmer Denis. Besides missing 'her friends and Marks & Spencer', Suzy soon found that as a married Greek wife, she took very little priority in Denis' life: 'The mother-in-law comes first in the Greek family, the wife is third – after the dog.' Then came Kim, a 36-year-old Scottish lecturer's daughter, who fell in love with barman Yorgo, forced her own parents to pay him a four-figure dowry, before being routinely castigated by her new family-in-law for not speaking Greek.

So much for the Hellenic Idyll.

'Giving away' dates with famous celebrities was a *Cosmo* ruse. In the summer of 1986, readers could apply to date dancer Ashley Page, comic Griff Rhys Jones, or even Ken Livingstone via a competition in the magazine's pages.

But for those who had shunned the sun-hunt, didn't fancy a night out with Red Ken, but were still serious about finding a long-term partner, they were readily handing over their fortunes to the dispassionate logic of matchmaking machines. In the early 1980s, operations such as Dateline and new competitors such as Datalink were thriving. Having managed to buck the previous decade's complaints about the lack of efficacy of the service, Dateline was now part of the Association of British Introduction Agencies, a not-for-profit safety net that had been established by Dateline founder John Patterson to give consumers some kind of quality assurance. The profits were rolling in and Dateline could afford to take out full-page national newspaper and magazine adverts, which included 'a true love story', apparently detailing the roller-coaster romance of how one real-life couple had met. By now, the company was advertising a year's membership, which began when you sent off two first-class stamps and filled in a basic questionnaire that appeared in the advert, requiring you to select a photo of the kind of person you most desired; what personality type you considered yourself to be (options included clothes-conscious, family-type, or intellectual), and then what kind of activities and interests you liked to indulge in (options included pets, classical music and the ominous-sounding 'conversation'.) But it still found itself having to assert that it was the 'totally acceptable way to widen your horizons'.

Where most people went on dates was still pretty parochial. Pubs were doing a roaring trade. Teens tried to get it on at Macdonald's or the local shopping centre, modelled on the American mall, and popularised by John Hughes films. The dance hall had been replaced by the disco, although 'disco-daters' were the subject of much scorn. In a *Daily Mail* report from Pantiles, a late 1980s Surrey hotspot, club taboos for women were listed as 'Getting drunk; dancing around handbags, failing to respond wittily to clever chat-up lines, showing underwear – no matter how short the miniskirt – and being seen dancing to Rick Astley records.' For men, they were '. . . unbuttoned shirts, talking about sport, making sexists remarks, dropping trousers and wearing scruffy clothes – even jeans and T-shirts are disappearing.'

And then, of course, there was the anti-dating venue: the acid-house rave.

Acid house was a dance party movement born in Chicago's gay clubs, which created an egalitarian, trans-formative space, where, bolstered by the right kind of drugs and thick beats, you could experience an almighty communal high.

At its peak, acid house saw the biggest party ever, held in a disused aircraft hangar in Berkshire, attended by some eleven thousand people. The mainstream press, politicians and the government were quick to jump on this potentially anarchic mass movement as proof that Britain's next generation was made up of '10,000 drug-crazed youths' (to quote a scurrilous *Sun* headline).

Eventually, one doctor, Dr Stephen Evans of Sheffield University, who had conducted a youth census of five thou-sand sixteen- to nineteen-year-olds, went on the record to say that he thought the main appeal wasn't to take drugs at all but the opportunity to meet with other young people, potentially with a view to finding their future marriage partners. But as one nineteen-year-old interviewed by the *Daily Express* in 1989 put it, 'Strangers come up to you, grab your hand and ask your name and your hometown, then they hug you as if you had known them all your life.' But despite the bonding conversations that took place between the barely acquainted, it was more likely that you'd reminisce about Charlene and Scott's wedding on the Australian soap *Neighbours*, which was watched by some twenty million people in 1988, on a come-down than go about plotting your own.

The drug might have inspired euphoria but it didn't invoke mass orgies – or at least in all the anxiety fuelled by its ubiquity, the mainstream media missed a trick to investigate the unwanted pregnancies and 'ecstasy babies' born as a result.

Meanwhile, in Europe, a cavalcade of English soldiers at a German barracks used a national paper to help them seek 'penfriends'. The side note in the *Daily Mirror*'s advice column 'Marie' read: 'Young ladies between 18 and 30 are invited to write to four friends to cure what they describe as the "West Germany blues". You can write to them at this address. And the boys would appreciate a photo if possible.'

Women needed to entertain men with a photo. It couldn't have better anticipated the technological dating revolution that was to come.

Chapter Thirteen

The Nineties: Modem love

The 1950s might have marked the first dance of teen dating in America, but by the time the 1990s dawned, a new generation of sassy young women had become its choreographers. On the big screen, adaptions of classic romances such as *Clueless* and *Ten Things I Hate About You* and TV shows such as *Dawson's Creek* presented feisty female leads who expected the young men in their lives to love, pleasure, entertain and respect them. A new generation of young women were being brought up to seek equality in romantic relationships. Internet porn had not yet become the primary sex educator. If the 1960s had been an age in which the promise of greater personal liberty drove experimentation and kinship, the 1990s was the era of earned and learnt expectation. Androgynous fashion, riot grrl music and stronger sexual harassment laws, including the recognition of rape within marriage, made for a more even sexual spirit level.

Women over the age of sixty, meanwhile, were also rediscovering their own sex lives. In an article from the *Daily Mail* of 22 June 1991, the paper's medical correspondent Jenny Hope reported on how improved health care and HRT was improving the sexual libidos of women, while men were experiencing something called 'emancipatory impotence', a result of men failing to live up to their partner's increased sexual expectations.

In some ways, the phrase 'emancipatory impotence' could be said to characterise younger women's predicament too. Of course, as we've already seen, women had always dieted and contorted themselves into the perfect shape of the day. But a kaleidoscopic focus on image, fashion, and styling had brought all of this into sharp relief. Women seemed to be worrying more than ever that their bodies were simply not up to par. In 1991, a Gallop Poll survey done for *New Woman* magazine reported that 90 per cent of all women believed they were overweight, with women in casual relationships the most worried – 36 per cent admitted hiding their bodies from their partners in embarrassment. Sixty-eight per cent of the five hundred women polled admitted that 'fat held them back'.

But only, it seemed, if they came from Britain.

In 1991, the collapse of the Soviet Union brought a whole new meaning to the term 'international relations'. Women from Russia and satellite countries including the Czech Republic, Romania, and Hungary wanted out – and the easiest, most lucrative option was via marriage to Western countries with more stable economies. Despite the UK heading into its own recession, life in Blighty was still a better bet. From Anastasiadate.com, which was founded in 1993, to the Ukranian specialist Lady Foxy, a bounty of sites sprung up to cater for this new border-crossing demand.

For the women that embarked on the journey, it could only mean a better life. Some fell in love, some fell in gratitude and commitment. Some fell in communion with a passport and divorced soon after. The men who had the money made an investment that provided companionate dividends. While the whispers in local communities – 'he *bought* her'

– remained, it seemed that for some couples, this kind of arrangement really did bring happy-ever-after.

But by the end of the decade, the International Organisation for Migration was reporting that mail-order bride rackets were part of the Russian Federation's sex trade web, a web that had its threads firmly extended into the UK, with long, sinewy links back to the Mafia. By posting photos of women who were not registered with the agencies, such as film stars, but fashioning an online persona featuring the pictures anyway, the individuals operating the sites would move to establish contact with punters who would then hand over thousands of pounds before finding out they'd been duped.

Simultaneously, there were agencies arranging meet-ups by which the visiting men would meet, greet and have sex with the women before ultimately rejecting all of them, thus effectively acting as an elite escort agency.

Russia wasn't the only country exploiting the UK's relative financial prosperity.

Brazil, the Philippines and Colombia also provided fertile ground in which to sow cross-cultural marriage seeds.

But despite the thousands of British men using these resources, the public attitude remained disapprovingly sanctimonious, and by the end of the decade the *Daily Express* had sought to humiliate the 75-year-old Chairman of Northern Gas, Brian Clegg, for his decision to order in a 23-year-old Thai bride. Details of the report included the fact that she could not speak English, and that Clegg knew no details of her previous life. Defending his decision, Clegg said, 'Some people might think I am just a dirty old man wanting to have sex with a girl. I was not after someone to be a mother to my son, but more a big sister for him. And apart from that, everyone likes a 23-year-old girl, don't they?'

Still, something in the sophistication of the practice of procuring mail-order brides was changing. Such was the stigma attached to the process that organisations offering the service were desperate to rebrand themselves, focusing on their role as 'international introduction' agencies, where highly educated, extremely beautiful women could meet eligible, solvent men. By the end of the decade, 'mail-order brides' had become 'international dating partners', with the advent of technology only aiding the public relations renaming. In 2013, the market research firm Experian estimated that the top ten international dating agencies had attracted more than twelve million visitors.

Some men, meanwhile, had anything but marriage on the brain. Since etiquette guides had died away at the beginning of the twentieth century, men didn't seem to have mainstream access to advice on relationships at all, and despite the best efforts of *Cosmo Man* which lasted for one issue, the launch of *Arena* in 1986, followed by *GQ* in 1989, and then *Esquire* in 1991, the conclusion had been that men simply couldn't be sold advice. They would, instead, revert to stealing it from women's magazines, or somehow muddle through.

This may explain why *Loaded* magazine, which launched in 1994, and contained absolutely no dating advice whatsoever, turned out to be a hit. The magazine 'for men who should know better' was soon selling nearly half a million copies a month, filled with features on the latest Page Three girl, soap totty, and letters from readers begging questions such as 'Why didn't you drug Kylie and strip her naked, we wouldn't have told her?' *Loaded* ran adverts from companies such as Jeans C17, featuring a model saying 'No, it's alright. You don't have to buy me dinner before I'll sleep with you.' Meanwhile, the Classified pages were a-brim with adverts for eighteen to thirties holidays promising singles and couples sex, pheromone sprays, sex education videos, ninety-pence-a-minute phone numbers for all kinds of chat lines, including 'Penis masturbation methods explained' and multiple gay chat lines. An antidote to the more sophisticated men's titles such as *Arena* and *GQ*, *Loaded* was aimed fairly and squarely at the Lad, a new personality type who stood as a combination antidote to the yuppy, New Romantic and New Man rolled into one. He drank too much, and revelled in his bad behaviour while intoxicated, treated women with uncouth, objectifying flippancy, had absolutely no interest in intimacy or committed relationships, revelled in his working-class roots, and occupied a position in the public eye that was at once reviled and minorly revered. His date was the Ladette, a woman who, in the words of journalist Victoria Coren, writing in the *Mail* in 1996, 'does her best to swear, leer and belch with the best of them', and was epitomised by the likes of TV presenters including Zoe Ball, Sara Cox and Denise Van Outen.

By 1998, Mori had conducted a poll on the outrageous behaviour of the nation's females, concluding that more women than ever before were embracing a free drinking, free attachment culture. And when writer Julie Burchill composed the ladettes' eulogy two years later, she identified the real hook beyond the pants-swapping dopamine-chase: 'In the Ladette, a man got the best of both worlds: a mate who he could drink and carouse with, and who'd give him a good seeing-to after the pubs closed . . . it may well be the case that the single life simply suits women, emotionally and physically, better than married life does – something which has never been true of men.'

Burchill had hit on a much-hidden home truth. While women's career prospects and life satisfaction frequently floundered upon marriage, men's prospered, culminating in everything from greater earning power to longer life expectancy once the knot had been tied. The Ladette, eyeliner smudged and dignity shredded as she might appear, was a luminous threat to the sexual status quo. No, single women need get no ideas.

But if there was one woman who proved that navigating single life was not the halcyon voyage Burchill identified it to be, it was Bridget Jones.

Helen Fielding's quixotic singleton first materialised as a character in a column for the *Independent* in the mid-1990s before she made her paperback debut a year or two later.

Fictional though she may have been, her travails, mainly circling around dieting, lack of career progress and her inability to find a reliant partner, resonated with scores of female readers, and soon Bridget's tag lines such as her 'v good' self-score, referencing how many calories, wine or bad men she'd managed to keep at bay, had become self-knowing shorthand used by a generation of female commentators who embraced Bridget as a sister-in-arms.

By the time the book had sold one million copies and been turned into a feature film, it had also inadvertently spawned a new genre of confessional writing, which columnists such as the *Telegraph*'s Bryony Gordon and the

Daily Mail's Liz Jones had mastered with candid aplomb. Out was the Helen Gurley Brown school of pin-thin perfectionism; in was Jones's confessions of sperm-stealing in the middle of the night in a desperate bid to get pregnant. Bridget's legacy was to allow thirty-something women to not have their shit together. And to voice it.

On the other side of the Atlantic stood Bridget's glossier cousin coven, the *Sex and the City* girls, who introduced a captive generation to, amongst other things, the rampant Rabbit vibrator. Every episode failed the Bechdel test – an on-screen assessment to decide whether the characters' sole conversational focus is men – and yet its central message – that the value of female friendship outweighed every other romantic relationship – was an essentially feminist one.

What Bridget and Miranda, Carrie, Samantha and Charlotte had in common then was that they embodied third-wave feminism, its newest and more nuanced incarnation which had more to say about women's struggle with body image, their ebbing fertility, their financial and career travails, and even that perhaps there were after all a few innate differences between men and women – and that this wasn't necessarily a bad or irreconcilable thing.

But for every feminist campaigner, such as Natasha Walter or bell hooks, who was fighting for better female equality in dating relationships, there were others keen to emphasise a more intuitive process. When the now infamous handbook *Women are from Venus, Men are from Mars* was first released in 1992, it struck a gender-specific nerve, and went on to become the highest ranked work of non-fiction of the 1990s, selling more than fifty million copies.

It seemed to offer an explanation to the 'anti-dating' that was rife in the 1990s, and its wisdom, generated by a male relationship coach, was apparently gleaned directly in the therapy room. Its essential premise was to identify and explain the preferred communicative strategies of men and women to one another, pointing out men's need for space and silence, as opposed to women's need for conversation and communion: 'When she says "I feel like you are not even here," he says "What do you mean I'm not here? Of course I am here. Don't you see my body?" '

Then in 1995, two unknown dating strategists published *The Rules*, a white-and-gold-bound imitation bible, which offered, not merely to close the Mars/Venus gap, but to have your man planet-hopping. As the authors explained, 'Nineties women simply have not been schooled in the basics.' It was an utter hit.

'The Rules' were split into thirty-five clauses, and included things such as 'Don't see him more than once or twice a week', 'Be honest but mysterious', and 'Stop dating him if he doesn't buy you a romantic gift for your birthday or Valentine's day', with a general overall message of making oneself as unavailable and elusive as possible in order to stoke maximum attentiveness and attraction.

The tone was mildly combative, the effect was, allegedly, deleterious, at least on men's ability to resist the women resisting them.

It certainly managed to address the problem that Wendy Dennis, author of an analysis of 1990s dating, had managed to identify in her tome *Hot and Bothered* – that 'the contemporary reality is that two people are out on a date, but no one will admit that a date is what they're out on'.

But if power play between the sexes levelled itself when they both played hard to get, it was set against a backdrop of political affairs where the getting resulted in some serious hard home truths.

Just as the Profumo affair exposed the hypocrisy around class, race and female emancipation in the 1960s, these new high-profile affairs – David Mellor and Antonia de Sanchez in the UK, and Bill Clinton and Monica Lewinsky in the US – demonstrated what liberties were not yet won for those who misbehaved in office, and the women that affronted them. No matter that women now had equal pay and sexual harassment laws. The message was nonetheless clear – women who dally with men who have power will come to bear their sexual shame.

But if there was one space where sexual shame was at least temporarily absolved, and anxieties about dating rituals allayed, it was in cyberspace.

In 1997, an online show entitled *Computer Chronicles*, run by the PBS broadcaster, began to feature a love online segment. Devised as an instructional item rather than reportage, it covered everything from chat rooms, computer matched dating, and 'blind date' websites (the text version of Chatroulette), plus 'the Cyrano server', an online scribe which would help you woo – or dump – a lover by composing you the perfect missive.

Today, the technology seems so basic, the sites featured look as though they've been composed on a Spirograph. But nonetheless, sites like the Cyrano server demonstrated how the internet could salve our endless and ancient appetites for the key to finding true love in yet another innovative way.

The year 1997 was also when AOL launched its Instant Messenger, which turned out to be an instant hit, and with nineteen thousand chat rooms, a veritable Pandora's box of interconnectivity amongst the handles and acronyms.

A year later came Yahoo! Messenger followed by MSN Messenger in 1999. Flirtation was evolving with every ping.

Chat-room conversations were soon the subject of newspaper and TV sketches. They injected a new level of excitement into romantic connection because of the lack of visibility of their participants, their semi-lawlessness. Sites such as Gaydar, the largest LGBT dating site, which launched in 1999 and had a major positive impact on gay connections around the world, helped LGBT individuals, and those into kink or non-conventional sexual practises, establish connections where to do so in public ran legal or socially ostracising risks. After all, it was only in 1992 that the World Health Organisation had declassified same-sex attraction as a mental illness and many countries still carried heavy penalties for those caught engaging in homosexual acts.

In Britain, the 90s was a heady time for LGBT rights. At the beginning of the decade, following the murder of five gay men, the organisation OutRage was set up to encourage the police to protect rather than target them. Meanwhile MPs determinedly fought the House of Lords for a levelling of the age limits for homosexual and heterosexual sex.

At the same time, the effect of increased gay visibility in popular culture in the 90s cannot be underestimated. Whether it was Ellen de Generes' coming out on The Ellen Show in 1997, or an anxious debate that Teletubby Tinky Winky might be in fact gay, the public conversation had changed. And while the steps to visibility were sometimes tentative – take the character of Smithers in the Simpsons, who started out as suggestively camp in early episodes before being fully 'outed' by scriptwriters in the Noughties – they meant that gays could never be stuffed back into the closet, even if there would still be violence, emotional pain, and political slander to deal with in the meantime.

By the end of the decade, in the UK, Channel 4 had broadcast Queer As Folk, a ground-breaking hit drama series about a trio of gay men in Manchester, radical for its nuanced depiction of their personal relationships and interactions.

But while stories of gay life in British cities were being beamed into British homes, most of the meeting was now taking place on the internet. Acronyms such as M4M (men for men) and W4W (women for women) were created and often attached to cities in order to create non-explicit geographically located access to other LGBT individuals without fear of reprimand. What's more, given the low grade of the available tech, it was not possible to routinely share photos digitally, which added simultaneously a certain frisson to proceedings, and more risk. Instead, the trick was to refine your practice of 'Cybering' – sexually stimulating the participant in your conversation by way of graphic description.

Anonymity came with its own problems. Today, it's simply not so easy to fake an online persona. The benefit to having multiple social media profiles, plus the ease by which you can search for a picture on Google, mean it's relatively easy to spot a fraud.

But without pictures, and without verifiable personal data, the internet's semi-lawlessness rendered it the perfect grooming ground for those wishing to take advantage of the young and vulnerable. By the end of the decade, teenage girls in particular had been pinpointed as the victims of these creepers. The *Daily Express* ran an in-depth report on the case of one young American girl called Katie who had been befriended by an online pal called Mark, 'nothing like the teenage boys she knew'. Before long, she'd flown out to meet him, discovered he was forty-one, and closely avoided a rape. He was prosecuted under the Communications Decency Act of 1996, a US Federal law that prohibits adults from using the internet to entice a minor into sex. Meanwhile, it would take the UK another seven years to come up with its own equivalent law, the 2003 Sexual Offences Act.

That might be the dramatic end of the wedge. It wasn't long before another more prosaic and predictable problem of chat-room surfing appeared – virtual infidelity. Individuals that had never previously sought out affairs or pornography now had these options at their fingertips. Soon therapists' consulting rooms were cradling couples who had discovered that one or the other was indulging in digital dangerous liaisons. The most obvious ways to detect this, came the professional therapeutic advice, was by what time people came to bed at night; if partners were getting in some online time early in the morning; protectiveness around computer passwords, credit card and telephone bills; and general defensiveness around computer use.

But by the end of the 1990s the limits of the cyber realm when it came to dating were also already becoming patently clear, and those of a more old-fashioned persuasion were eager for face-to-face, rather than interface, interactions.

In 1998, an LA-based rabbi called Yaacov Deyo hosted a group of friends at his home in California, asking them for ideas on how they could best serve the dating needs of the local Jewish community. They came up with the idea of a ten-minute table-hopping escapade that would give participants a quick and efficient way to assess their temporary date as a potential spouse. Using an Excel spreadsheet to keep track of the participants, along with feedback cards that recorded their impressions, they launched their experiment in a Peet's coffee house in Beverly Hills and began the process of patenting the notion of 'SpeedDating'. Within a year the experiment had exploded and Deyo gave up on the idea of trying to trademark it: 'In Judaism, there's a concept of *zechus* – the merit that is created by a good action,' he told the *New York Times* magazine in 2013. If the action was leading to more marriages and babies across the world, that was good enough for Deyo.

Yet despite its initial operative intentions, it wasn't always clear what the desired outcome of the speed-daters that joined the fray were. When it reached London, an undercover *Daily Express* report of a crew of twenty-somethings found that they believed they'd really got a sense of someone from first impressions. Did any of them believe speed-dating could lead to a long-term relationship? Did it matter? This was less about microwaving you a spouse, and more about taking you for a spin on a hot plate.

Speed-dating firmly attracted a young demographic, for whom the dating game was very much still that. But there was a new character to be catered for – the divorcee.

By 1994, divorces were at an all-time high, with the average age for men being thirty-eight and that for women, thirty-five. These were people with mortgages, careers, children – and the drive to meet, if not mate, once again. In just over a decade, more than 20 per cent of women over forty would be without a ring on it. 'Left on the shelf' no longer applied, argued the writer Marcelle D'argy Smith, when it seemed that women had merely re-seated themselves higher up the unit. But could divorced men be persuaded to see their value?

The problem seemed to be that middle-aged men sought younger women. Not just because they were firm of flesh, concluded Smith, but because they were sexually enthusiastic, could be more easily impressed by a forty-something-year-old male's achievements, didn't moan about former lovers, and were generally not cross with men and disenchanted with life.

As one attractive 46-year-old interviewed by the *Daily Mail* in 'an increasingly Nineties dilemma' ruminated, 'divorced men like the ones I met through the dating agency, have all turned out to be emotionally damaged, while the single ones are off-puttingly anxious and eager to please'.

It would be another decade before the term 'cougar' and the concept of cougar dating truly entered the lexicon. In the meantime, older English women upped the Shirley Valentine stakes by embarking on a new kind of sex tourism – adventures to Africa and the Caribbean where young native 'rastitutes' lay awaiting to take them to sexual heaven, via the cash point. Press reports focused on the desperation of both parties, and between 2002 and 2003, authorities in Gambia even tried to clear the beaches of the enabling young men.

Meanwhile, for those that decided to stick it out with their English male contemporaries, there was one serious, secret downside – impotency. And then, as if just in time to deal with the 1990s bounty, in 1998, a small blue pill appeared on the dating scene. In some ways it was to later-age dating what ecstasy had been to the acid-house crew, in part because it was similarly procured under the counter by millions once its effects had become known. Its name? Sildenafil. Otherwise known as Viagra.

Viagra was, as many drugs are, an accidental invention. Originally developed in the UK for the treatment of angina, the discovery that it could assist men with erectile dysfunction problems meant that it was hailed as a wonder drug, the kind doctors such as Irwin Goldstein, Professor of Urology at Boston University Medical School had dreamed of. It was not an aphrodisiac, only being effective when a man was sexually stimulated, but by improving and prolonging erections via a single oral tablet, it was unlike any other substance that had been developed to treat impotency before.

The debate about the drug's availability bolstered the belief that the cure for impotency should be a privilege not a right, and support built up around the idea that NHS prescriptions for Viagra would be taking funding away from treatments for life-threatening conditions such as heart disease, cystic fibrosis and cancer. The estimate was that a prescription of just a single tablet a week for all who required it within one local authority would cost £700,000 a year.

Reports began to filter in that it could result in everything from damaged eyesight to death. What's more, there was a hidden cost to relationships. 'Women already think men are led too much by their anatomy' wrote the *New York Times* columnist Maureen Dowd. There was now the added complication of bruising female egos, lest they felt left out of the arousal process. And then came Britain's first 'Viagra divorce', in which a husband's unreasonable sexual demands were blamed on his taking the drug. This case of 'Viagramony' was, incidentally, one of nearly a hundred that had been recorded across the West by this point, by which Viagra was being directly blamed for wrecking relationships.

And then there were the young men who were wilfully experimenting with the drug as a mere performance enhancer, using it as a 'thrill pill' and, in the most risky cases, combining it with poppers, otherwise known as amyl nitrate, which could result in a sudden drop in blood pressure, leading to death.

Yet despite the media scare stories, the dating nightmares and divorces, most men and women were behaving more responsibly and respectfully than they ever had in their personal dating relationships, as the results from 1990s NATSAL went on to prove.

For one thing, they revealed that monogamy within cohabitation was treated just as seriously as monogamy within marriage, with 77 per cent of women and 85 per cent of men believing infidelity to be wrong. Similarly, although one-night stands were now more tolerated than they had been a decade before, sex outside of a relationship, even where the couple didn't live together, was now 10 per cent more frowned upon. And while the marriage rate had declined by nearly 10 per cent over the decade, it seemed that young men who did commit were more willing to demonstrate that commitment, as evidenced by an article that appeared in *GQ* magazine, entitled 'Do Real Men Wear Wedding Rings?', with the majority who did, 73 per cent, aged between twenty-five and twenty-nine.

Millennium eve turned out to be the most popular of the century for marriage proposals, including those conducted over the internet. The course of true love had been irrevocably altered by the information super-highway. But for how much good?

Chapter Fourteen

The Noughties and now: Appy ever after?

'Modern women are refusing to commit to relationships.' So sounded the *Daily Mail*'s klaxon at the turn of the decade as it agonised over why ladies had stopped prioritising romance. The standfirst was decorated with the following panic-stricken tag lines – 'why women are leaving it too late to find a man', 'they prefer loneliness to a bad relationship', and 'why one in four might never become a mother'. But the women interviewed came across as confident, successful and content with their life choices. However much the right-wing press protested, women's own stories contradicted the panic. Motherhood and marriage were simply no longer the drivers of their dating behaviour, no matter the frenzy which American books such as *Marry Me!* attempted to engineer. Written by a male triumvirate who'd penned the previous best-selling *What Men Want*, this self-explanatory tome broke down the formula for securing marriage: 'Be patient, stay the same, understand his devotion to work = A PROPOSAL' and advised readers to understand that his career would come first, that you should never admit to having had more than ten sexual partners, to keep your emotional baggage at the door and to remember that sex means everything.

Yet at the same time there was an undercurrent of anxiety about the fact that women might have finally got exactly what they wanted, and that it was damaging them.

In October 2003, *Cosmopolitan* editor Lorraine Candy penned a concerned editor's letter about the rise in what she termed 'McSex': soulless sex which involved interaction with 'men they don't know and probably don't want to see again ... it's not what feminists fought for, and it's something we've never advocated in *Cosmo*'. The editorial prefaced an article on the rise of one-night stands – a depressing report from Friday nights across the country, littered with spilt drinks, split skirts, and absolutely no aspirations for love or commitment of any kind.

The piece was then quickly followed by a feature interviewing a thousand men between the ages of eighteen and thirty-five on what they considered to be an ideal first date.

The key findings from the survey were: that 79 per cent of men 'can't resist knee-high boots or stilettos'; that you should drink wine or champagne rather than lager; that 83 per cent of men viewed eye contact as a sign the woman they were on a date with was interested in them; that telling a joke would impress 90 per cent of them but wearing too much jewellery or having visible tattoos or piercings would be a turn-off for 79 per cent of them. Men were also more or less happy to pay for the date, but appreciated it if a woman offered to contribute.

Interestingly, 55 per cent of the men surveyed were allegedly looking for a long-term relationship.

Cosmo's bottom line was clear. The zipless fuck of Erica Jong's 1970s imagination had not yet materialised. Nor had the 'friends with benefits' concept yet filtered into the 'acceptable' sexual behaviour category, even if it was being practised in the bedrooms of *Cosmo* readers.

As it turned out, there was a weird strand of puritanism creeping into dating relations on the other side of the Atlantic. And it was having a ripple effect here. In the mid 2000s, the biggest dating craze to hit America was actually the purity movement, consisting of a cavalcade of teens and young twenty-somethings who pledged to remain virgins until marriage. With Britney Spears its poster-child (despite salacious rumours), the purity movement started in the 1980s in response to the Aids epidemic but was adopted by evangelical Christians, eager for an on-trend way to promote their modest virtues. Under the slogan of 'True love waits', couples exchanged chastity rings and pledged mutual virginity until they made it up the aisle, while oral and anal sex and mutual masturbation were also all technically forbidden. Meanwhile, accountability groups for the men and mentors for the women helped to guide them away from lustful thoughts and activities such as viewing pornography.

There were even purity balls held where girls made a pledge to remain chaste in front of their fathers, who made a counter-pledge to protect their daughter's virginity.

This went hand in hand with the practice of abstinence-only education which has been prevalent since the 2000s in the US, and eligible for government funding, (the feminist author Jessica Valenti estimates such education programmes have received more than $1.3 billion dollars since 1996), all despite evidence that such initiatives usually result in anything but abstinence.

Meanwhile in the UK, child psychology experts were ruminating over a lost age of innocence. In 2003, Esther Rantzen, the broadcaster and creator of Childline, expounded on the phenomenon of seven-year-olds enjoying a girlfriend or boyfriend. Examining research done by Dr

Emma Renold of Cardiff University, Rantzen ruminated on the fact that 'going steady, holding hands and even kissing' were being reported as common behaviours, obviously a result of children 'mimicking the world they see around them – a world in which lingerie manufacturers created padded bras for six-year-olds, and drinks companies design "alcopops" to introduce alcohol to children whose palates are still attuned to lemonade'.

One section of society, however, was finding its romantic feet like never before: the LGBT, now the LGBTQI community.

Throughout the 1980s and '90s, the pressure group Press for Change had campaigned for trans people to be allowed to marry. Then, in 2004, the UK government passed the Gender Recognition Act. As far back as the 1960s, it had been argued that birth certificates could be amended for the sake of inheritance, but this new legislation ensured that trans individuals were now granted full legal recognition in every aspect of law. By the end of the decade, 'gender reassignment' was a protected characteristic under the 2010 Equality Act, meaning that any individual who was undergoing or proposing to undergo any part of the process of reassignment and facing discrimination or abuse for it could seek protection under the law.

In 2000, the armed forces lifted the ban on LGBT people serving, then, in 2001, after repeated conflict with the House of Lords, the age of consent for homosexual sex was finally reduced from eighteen to sixteen. Revisions to the Human Rights Act also meant that gay rights for immigrants were more robust than ever. The pressure group Stonewall had been instrumental in forcing the then Home Secretary Michael Howard's hand on the issue of letting twenty immigrants into the UK purely on the basis that their British resident partner was gay. Then, in 2004, the Civil Partnership Act was passed, giving same-sex couples the same rights and responsibilities as married ones in England, Scotland, Northern Ireland and Wales.

It did not pass without controversy, and not merely from the expected Conservative quarters, who disapproved of anything even approximating marriage.

Instead, leading gay rights campaigner Peter Tatchell said it would lead to 'sexual apartheid' and opposed what he perceived to be creating a two-tier romancescape, one kind of partnership for straight couples and another for gay.

As it turned out, some 16,100 unions were formed in the first year they became legal with some straight couples wanting in on the act. By the end of the decade, a straight couple called Tom Freeman and Katherine Doyle had even petitioned for a civil partnership and been turned down by Islington registry office. In a public statement they expressed their dismay: 'In a democratic state, all institutions should be open to all people.' And so the battle would continue until in 2014 the UK government finally passed legislations legalising gay marriage.

Partnership rights aside, there was still the matter of finding one's happily-ever-after. Finally, one locale had outstripped the dance hall. It was cyberspace.

Instant chat fatigue had not yet set in, and the dot.com boom of the late 1990s had exploded the opportunities for dating-related outfits, spawned social networking, and created a dozen communicative tools that would only expand and enhance the possibilities for intimate interactions.

Both Skype and Myspace launched in 2003, the latter with the purpose of allowing users to create their own virtual club page from which they could share their tastes and predilections. But savvy net users soon began to share tips on how to utilise the site as a free dating service, with programmes such as DatingAnyone being launched that could comb the site for changes in relationship status, giving you the opportunity to pounce on the newly single or rebounding. It was cyber-stalking, done legitimately.

Once Facebook had successfully launched in 2004, the bar for social networking sites and their scope for romantic introductions and relationships had been set. In 2007, a software engineer called John Baku launched a site called FriendswithFetishes. It would go on to be renamed FetLife and become the single largest online community for those of a kinky persuasion. To this day, it remains relatively unchallenged as an online space for those of a non-vanilla persuasion to share fantasies, and meet – or not – in the flesh.

And then came the threat – or promise – of virtual reality. In 2003, a San Francisco-based tech company called Linden Lab devised Second Life, a virtual world that allows users to voyage into a fantasyscape by which they can meet, fuck, marry, tarry, kill and experiment with just about any kind of sexual behaviour they might refrain from in real life. In 2008, it was reported that a British couple, Amy Taylor and David Pollard, were to divorce because of the husband's Second Life affairs. Falling for another avatar, claimed the wife, was still cheating.

But it wasn't just SL causing problems. With the invention of broadband internet had come the proliferation of internet porn, and its connected live shows and chat rooms. Suddenly fidelity had a new bandwidth and not a week went by without a media outlet posing the question, 'Is porn cheating?'

Soon, women and men were confessing to an increased performance anxiety caused by the spectre of adult content in their bedrooms. While the debate around the technicalities of whether you could actually be addicted to porn in the same way you could be addicted to cocaine vacillated, by the end of the decade the jury was more or less unanimous – too much porn was not good for your core relationship.

But the democratisation of porn access had done something else. Simultaneously, it had narrowed and widened the gulf between fantasy and reality. The women that populated chat rooms and poolsides and dungeons were hyper-real. Ever-ready, ever-enthusiastic, ever-searchable. They did not need to be chatted up to be sexually engaged. This was not helping men's offline skills with the opposite sex.

Instead, the internet's privacy, anonymity, and suitability for men who were better at looking at pictures or talking in binary than the language of seduction made it the perfect tool by which they could stalk, lure and attempt to woo women. Men had rarely wanted to discuss dating in a public forum, too keen not to lose face, but online, they couldn't wait to skill up, compare notes and compete over QWERTY. They ruminated together in chat rooms and forums dedicated to seduction techniques where they could share tips, and express a frustrated misogyny as to why the women of their dreams always seemed to go for the jocks and jerks of this world.

But ruminating on the internet was only ever going to be so satisfying.

You might be able to get her to agree to a date, but what did you do once you finally had her there before you in the flesh? Men needed a game plan. Cue – *The Game*.

Originally an autobiographical tale of Neil Strauss's embroilment in the Pick Up Artist (PUA) movement, which aimed to develop a range of fail-proof pulling tactics for awkward men to use on low-self-esteemed women, *The Game* soon morphed into a handbook of its own, spreading the techniques popularised by Mystery, Ross Jeffries and the other PUAs profiled to a new audience. These techniques include 'sarging', whereby you actively cruise for women and make a written note of any hotties you find; the Neg – giving a woman a backhanded compliment which will see her craving your positive attention, such as 'great nails – are they fake?'; and Kino – whereby you briefly touch a woman you're trying to hook up with in order to stimulate her desire for physical connection.

As Strauss himself put it, 'The sell is that, with the special techniques they learn from Mystery and other gurus, the uber-geeky can often give a convincing simulation of being a regular human being, even if [. . .] they are in fact sociopaths.'

Yet although it was rapidly observed that 'gaming' was essentially the preserve of men without charisma, social skills, or high self-esteem themselves, the book sold more than two million copies, spawned a spin-off, *The Rules of the Game*, and infiltrated dating culture as a key means of securing female attention. It has taken a decade for the tide to turn against the PUA movement and although it maintains a presence, as proven by continuing sales of the books and the popularity of websites such as Return of Kings, a watershed was marked in May 2014 when a

22-year-old Santa Barbara university student called Eliot Rodger opened fire on his classmates in Isla Vista, following his rejection by a female student he had been fruitlessly pursuing. When pick-up artist Julien Blanc wanted to come and tout his manipulation-soaked tricks to bevies of wannabe studs in the UK six months later, he was refused a tourist visa. Blanc may not have advocated for Rodger, but the image of pick-up artistry as harmless persuasion had been sullied for good.

In 2015, Strauss published *The Truth* in which he set out to do penance for *The Game*. In it, he describes how after ten years of sleeping his way around California and anywhere else his spin took him, he finally checked himself into a sex addiction clinic for failing to stop compulsively cheating on the woman who would later become his wife. Strauss's story is a cautionary tale and an apology of sorts for all the amateur pick-up artists his original book spawned. Besides, as Strauss observed in interview with the *Guardian* in October 2015, it was the pick-up artists themselves that were being conned: 'I think that a lot of guys who read *The Game*, they think that they're fooling or tricking women. But most women are smart enough to know exactly what you're doing. They just might like you enough to go along with it.'

At the same time, women were not immune from 'gaming' themselves, and indulging their own online fantasy lives. When a work of self-published *Twilight*-inspired erotica began to do the digital rounds in 2011, it soon became a cult hit. Some thirty thousand downloads later, it was snapped up for a cool one million pounds by Random House. Mr Christian Grey would see to us all now.

Fifty Shades was by no means the first erotic novel to sensually grip the female sexual imagination. But its ubiquity has made it more than a mere international publishing phenomenon. The so-called '*Fifty Shades* effect' (which caused erotic fiction in general to 'cannibalise' the rest of the UK book market, according to the *Bookseller* in 2012) saw sales of pleasure products rocket and fetish nights at previously dilettante clubs boom, while visitors to adult site PornHub searched for BDSM content featuring 'submission' by an increase of 55 per cent.

At the same time there was a deeper social panic incited by the birth of so-called 'mommy porn'. While conservative naysayers ruminated about everything from its possible effect on STI rates to sexual violence against women, many a middle-aged man began to feel he couldn't compete with the literary stud his partner had brought to bed. Then, in a feature for *Newsweek*, Katie Roiphe pondered this 'stylized theatre of female powerlessness' and concluded that it was a subtle reaction to the powers afforded women by feminism, rather than evidence that women had never been afforded true sexual equality in the first place. So what if more women on more dating sites were advertising for Grey-alike boyfriends? This was not simply self-flagellatory flagellation, but a chance for kink-inclined women to come out of the closet, cuffs in hand.

Still, women seeking men to do intricate things to them with rope and cable ties was never going to be the game that captured the public's dating imagination. Instead, it would take a much simpler premise – hot or not matches that were potentially up for some adult fun that night – to ensnare a new generation of lovers.

'We always saw Tinder, the interface, as a game', said Tinder co-founder Sean Rad commenting in *Time* magazine in 2014. And it's that gaming aspect that has fuelled the fire of its users' addiction to it, with some 850 million swipes taking place around the world each day.

Invented in 2011 by two University of Southern California undergraduates named Sean Rad and Justin Mateen, the app launched at a college party there before extending its lascivious pixels to other college campuses soon after. By October 2014, the app had more than fifty million users, average age twenty-seven, with the company valued at nearly $1billion.

Tinder's success rests on its brazen efficiency. If you are one of the few people who haven't downloaded it out of curiosity, here's the lowdown: it functions by showing you a single photo at a time of a potential match. You then swipe the picture with your thumb – left if you want to discard them or right if you want to make a match. If they have also right-swiped you, you receive notification and are then able to 'chat'. You can also 'super-like' someone to combat the ubiquity of the right swipe and hammer your infatuation home. Inspired by the gay dating app Grindr, the whole premise of making a snap physical judgement, expressing that interest and then chatting to your chosen hottie if there is a mutual interest has whittled the courtship process down to its Neanderthalic essentials and even invited the term Tinderitis – repetitive strain injury caused by too much right-thumbed swiping – which has now slipped into common parlance.

In essence the process is no different to the one we go through when selecting a partner across a crowded bar or party. Rather, the virtual venue just features greatly extended perimeters. But the notion of the 'Tinder Generation' has generated all kinds of conservative and liberal concern alike over how it is changing relationships for the worse. In particular, researchers have focused on the Choice Effect; the notion that too many options are paralysing us, and hampering our ability to commit as we remain constantly on the lookout for an upgrade.

But apps like Tinder also have an entertainment function, and it's not infrequent for groups of users to 'play' together with no intention of hooking up or even meeting up with any of the other users whose profiles they peruse. If the use of smartphones encourages insularity on the one hand, we are finding a cooperative way to compensate for it and including others in our search for the perfect partner, despite the individualistic freedom posed by modern technology. Tinder has also inspired Instagram and Reddit feeds, which feature the mad, bad and downright ugliest messages that have passed back and forth for the entertainment of all online. In the social media age, it's become easier than ever to ridicule those who don't have the requisite social and emotional skills to score at scoring.

Since Tinder shimmied onto the market, there have been dozens of other dating apps launched. Happn flags up people you cross paths with. 3nder allows you to match with singles and couples for kinky experiences. Bumble allows women – and only women – to send the first message to a male recipient. Pitting itself as the anti-Tinder, Coffee Meets Bagel offers users just a single match a day. HowAboutWe matches users based on their hobbies, interests, and where they like to hang out. And then there's Double, which advertises you along with a friend or wingman. Meanwhile Snapchat, which allows users to send unique photos and videos for a limited time, is a key part of millennial courtship.

Meanwhile, Tinder's ambitions are far-reaching: it wants to become more like the social networking app it borrows data from – Facebook – so that it has something to offer its already-coupled users as well as its single players. Dating apps have so far targeted our hunt for the perfect partner – but once we find that partner, what functionality could they have for us then? Date-venue suggestions, sex tips, wedding planning apps have all featured but none have captured the popular imagination like those that facilitate The Hunt.

If the Buccaneer brides of the 1900s had to set sail for England for good, it's also never been easier to explore one's international options. All major dating websites now allow us to search by geographical location, and while the feature is essentially designed to harness the power of proximity, it's entirely possible to select a faraway land in which to quest for a partner. What's more, given the location facility of dating apps, venturing abroad usually automatically generates a new pool of potential suitors, for however long you might reside in a new locale.

What's more, technology is evolving to facilitate even more ways for you to keep love across borders alive. Take the rise of teledildonics – the name for interactive sex toys that allow couples to connect physically by remote operation. Originally conceived by the adult industry as a way for cunt-struck fans to get several bytes closer to their favourite porn stars, toys such as the OhMiBod music-stimulated massager, or the Kiiroo Onyx and Pearl sleeve masturbator and dildo set have become popular as a couples toy. They work by allowing one partner to operate a device worn by the other via Wi-Fi or Bluetooth, operational by computer, tablet or smartphone. Integrated video chat helps to make the experience even more intimate.

Virtual Reality is also in the process of being optimised to create extra-dimensional dating opportunities. Second Life may have suffered from something of a stillbirth but VR has been given a new lease of life, thanks to the developers of Oculus Rift, who envisage a product that will connect lovers in their own other-dimensional game.

Meanwhile, if the age of mainstream TV viewing is over, the age of TV dating shows is definitely not. From *First Dates* to *The Undateables*, to *Love Island*, to *Sex Box*, the last salacious instalment in our entertainment schedules is *Naked Attraction*, in which participants select each other based solely on their body parts.

While these kinds of programmes uphold the boy meets girl status quo, the most significant shift for dating seems to be the fact non-gender binary love is on the horizon as a dating norm.

If the internet has transformed the sheer scope by which we can hook up, it is obvious but nonetheless vital to say that it has transformed the means by which people self-define their own sexuality. If you were bi or transsexual, a balloon fetishist, or into pony play fifty years ago, you had to take your chances with a heavily coded message in an underground sex mag.

These days, you simply Google your preference. Those with an unconventional sexuality have never been able to seek one another out with such ease or granularity. But it goes deeper than that. The variety of sex and relationships we read about on the internet are influencing the scope of what we consider possible. We are becoming more sexually fluid, more likely to experiment with gender, genitals, props or power, and less likely to see the need to label it. And it's generational. A YouGov poll from 2015 found that only 46 per cent of 18- to 24-year-olds would define themselves as exclusively heterosexual.

In particular, the rise of transgender identity has had a subtle yet critical effect on broadening our conceptions of sex and gender, and influencing how and who we love. From the candid comings-out of celebrities such as Laverne Cox and Caitlin Jenner, to the fictional depiction of a trans relationship in the BBC sitcom *Boy Meets Girl*, we are suddenly seeing trans men and women as more than just the reductive, pornographic sum of their body parts.

And if categories of boy versus girl are ceasing to matter, that can only have a positive effect for sexual equality and self-expression as a whole. Case in point: CoverGirl recently appointed their first male spokesperson, a seventeen-year-old US high school senior and make-up artist named James Charles whose meticulously painted face belies gender conformity.

When it comes to alternative sexualities, celebrity 'outings' are crucial for giving the hesitant encouraging role models and increasing general acceptance. In the case of Olympic diver Tom Daley and model Cara Delevingne, two individuals who embody idealised representations of masculinity and femininity respectively, the message is clear: how you 'present' has no bearing on who you love.

What makes this wave of sexual fluidity different from the 1970s, however, is that it no longer goes hand in hand with so-called promiscuity.

STI rates, in particular diagnoses for HPV and gonorrhoea may be up, but that is partly attributable to a greater attendance at sexual health clinics. Instead, younger people are increasingly responsible. They don't drink, take drugs or get pregnant at the same rate as their parents and grandparents. While the cost of weddings has increased, the recession has forced many couples into premature cohabitation, or back to their parents' homes. Rent increases have forced the closure of underground gay clubs, while fast-food restaurant Nando's has become the UK's most popular venue for a date. A lack of not only disposable income but permanent jobs offering progression and stabilising benefits has had a deleterious effect on millennials' short-term habits and long-term expectations.

With so many curtailing pressures put upon millennial relationships, this may also partly explain why ethical non-monogamy is no longer the mere preserve of 1970s San Franciscans. If monogamy is no longer cherished for its role in ensuring inheritance rights, it's becoming an increasingly popular option for those who might once have played the field for longer but simply cannot afford financially to do so. Now a designated relationship choice more and more frequently practised by discreet suburban types, it's also more likely to be slipped into a mainstream dating profile. Similarly, if sex parties were once the preserve of 1960s rebels and revolutionaries, they are now more likely to be part of a couple's early experimentation. Elite sex party Killing Kittens, for example, has now been going for more than ten years, and attracts a bevvy of securely attached, toned-bodied twenty- and thirty-somethings.

At the same time, the rise and ubiquity of celebrity gossip sites mean we've never been so heavily influenced by starry relationships. From Kimye's stadium proposal and Tuscan wedding to Brangelina's divorce, celebrity couples carry more soft power together than apart. Their relationship with the brands that mate with them in turn influences our own relationships.

And in their wanton display of perfectly filtered love, so our own social media behaviour follows suit. We share more and more about our sweeties because we want to be regarded for our emotional intelligence, stability and ability to attract a killer mate. The 'relationshipgoals' hashtag on Instagram, the photo album app which allows users to share pictures with the world, has been used more than three million times.

Given the hold tech has on our psyches as well as our behaviour, it's inevitable that the dating game has come to look just like mobile gaming. But at the same time there has been a resurgence in bespoke matchmaking. A few years ago, I moonlighted as a matcher and dating coach in Silicon Valley for a matchmaking start-up. Like most start-ups, it never got off the ground, but the experience reassured me that most people, at heart, are looking to find that single special someone.

Since I was working in the Bay Area, some of the requirements seemed outrageously Californian to my English sensibilities. Take the Russian-born female realtor who had quickly assimilated into the health-conscious culture: 'He has to be tall, tanned, weight no more than 140 pounds. Be able to lift me up with no effort. Be vegan, drink kombucha and take vitamins. And to have good energy. I will have nobody bringing crazy or down energy into my house.'

In addition to this list, she informed me, she needed someone with manners, who was ready to start a family. 'I'm so over hook-up culture. I'm thirty-seven. It's time to get real.' So when I told her I had the perfect, fit, handsome, ready-for-fatherhood twenty-something bodied yet old-fashioned mannered gent who hadn't gotten jiggy in five years because he preferred connected sex with someone he loved to a casual hook-up, I braced myself for a bear hug. Instead, she was horrified. 'Oh no. Celibate for FIVE YEARS? That's just flat-out weird.'

What no dating app or matchmaking service can predict, of course, is chemistry. Only, there is a way to harness the match power of pheromones. In 1995, an experiment conducted at the University of Bern devised something called the 'sweaty T-shirt test', whereby women were asked to smell well-sweated into garments worn by men. The discovery was that women were consistently attracted to immune systems that differed from their own.

And now a site called Smell Dating has recently devised what it calls the first mail odour dating service. It serves participants by sending them a T-shirt by mail order, which they wear for three days before returning it to the organisation. In turn, they receive samples of other candidates' T-shirts. Candidates then select one another on the basis of smell preference. It considers this a first port of call for making a dating-based decision. After all, a chemistry test obviously can't compensate for other factors – value difference such as religious or political beliefs for example, or previous relationship experience that would dictate someone's intimacy blocks, paranoia about divorce, or clingy tendencies.

But online dating is now the norm, and, if statistics are to be believed, the most reliable way to meet a partner. In a study commissioned by dating site eHarmony, a survey of 19,131 people found that couples who met online were less likely to get divorced or separated, and more likely to report relationship satisfaction.

Compare the sheer variety of today's internet dating sites with Victorian matrimonial papers and the criteria by which to select a mate have crystallised beyond belief. Jewish dating, Christian dating, gamer dating, single-parent dating, dog-lovers dating, uniform-wearers dating, Asperger's dating . . . these are just a sliver of the options available to us in the year 2017.

After all, dating is the new wedlock. Marriage is at its lowest level since 1895. Despite the sporadic surveys announcing that married people live longer (if more unhappily along the way), marriage just doesn't seem to be fit for twenty-first century purpose any more. But dating? Dating has a diamond-bright future.

Bibliography

BOOKS

Allbutt, H, (1894), *The Wife's Handbook,* R Forder

Anon, (1879), *The Worcester Letter Writer*, Dick and Fitzgerald

Anon, (1894), *Raped on the Railway,* Charles Carrington

Armstrong, Lucie Heaton, (1903), *Good Form,* Reinkin

Austen, Jane, (2003) *Pride and Prejudice*, Penguin

Austen, Jane, (2007) *Persuasion,* Penguin

Berkoff, Steven, (1997), *Free Association,* Faber and Faber

Besant, Annie, (1877), *The Law of Population,* Freethought Publishing Co.

De Beauvoir, Simone, (2014), *The Second Sex,* Vintage

Bindel, Julie, (2014), *Straight Expectations*, Guardian Books

Carpenter, Edward, (2015), *The Intermediate Sex,* Routledge

Comfort, Alex, (1974), *The Joy of Sex,* Quartet Books

Conran, Shirley, (1986), *Lace,* Penguin

Cruikshank, Dan, (2009), *The Secret History of Georgian London,* Random House

Dennis, Peter, (1992), *Daring Hearts,* Queen Spark

Dennis, Wendy, (1993), *Hot and Bothered,* Grafton

Eyles, Leonara, (1964), *Sex for the Engaged,* Hale

Fielding, Helen, (2016), *The Diary of Bridget Jones,* Picador

Forel, August, (1927), *The Sexual Question,* Heinemann

Gorer, Geoffrey, (2014), *Exploring English Character*, Nabu Press

Gray, John, (2012), *Men are from Mars, Women Are From Venus,* Harper Element

Griffiths, Edward, (1947), *Modern Marriage*, Methuen

Gurley Brown, Helen, (2003), *Sex and the Single Girl*, Barricade Books

Greer, Germaine, (2008), *The Female Eunuch*, Harper Perennial

Haste, Cate, (2002), *Rules of Desire*, Vintage

Hall, Radclyffe, (1990), *The Well of Loneliness*, Anchor

Hillis, Marjorie, (2008), *How to live alone and like it*, 5 Spot

Hogg and Brown, *The Complete Letter-writer* (1800), Hogg

Reeves, J H, (1886), *Reeves Pocket Companion*, J. H Reeves

Schofield, Michael (1968), *The Sexual Behaviour of Young People*, Penguin

Stopes, Marie, (1943), *Married Love*, Putnam and Co.

Stopes, Marie, (1951), *Wise Parenthood*, Putnam and Co.

Strauss, Neil, (2008), *The Game*, Canongate Books

Strauss, (2016), *The Truth*, Canongate Books

Valenti, Jessica, (2010), *The Purity Myth*, Seal Press

Van de Velde, Theodoor Hendrik, (1965), *Ideal Marriage*, William Heinemann Medical Books

JOURNALS, MAGAZINES AND NEWSPAPERS

Forum magazine, 1966–1974

Ladies Home Journal, from 1907

Woman's Weekly, 1914

The Adult

The Link

T.P's Weekly

Matrimonial News

Matrimonial Gazette

The Queen

Lilliput (1935)

London Life

Time and Tide magazine (1935)

Woman magazine

Men-only magazine (1935)

Lilliput (1937)

Articles

Roiphe, Katie, 'Working Women's Fantasies', *Newsweek*, April 2012

Stampler, Laura, 'Inside Tinder: Meet The Guys Who Turned Dating Into An Addiction,' *Time* magazine, February 2014

Norris, Kathleen, 'The Kind of Girl I Want My Son To Marry', *Good Housekeeping*, 1930

Lamont, Tom, Interview with Neil Strauss, the *Guardian*, October 2015

Anon, 'The Confessions of an Engaged Couple', *Ladies Home Journal*, 1907

Acknowledgements

When I began *The Curious History of Dating*, I had no conception of the depth of research needed to write it. But the staff at the British Library and the Wellcome Library calmly navigated me as I sought out the right resources.

My thanks go to my dad, my imagined reader, who isn't around to see the publication of this, but whose love of history, social justice, and the mischievous, inspired how I shaped the narrative and what quixotic gems I pulled out.

To my mum, who oh-so-gamely over-shared details for her own rite of sexual passage to enable my endeavours. For always believing I will reach the end even when I waver, and for teaching me to read in the first place, I love you.

To Dr Sarah Mansfield, whose support and steer enabled me to pluck up the courage to begin, and to finish.

To Zoe Apostolides, who saved the hour with her intellect, verve and cool-headedness.

To Victoria Seabrook who so expediently and conscientiously helped source additional material for the later chapters.

To my agent Lisa Moylett, a supportive pillar of smart glamour, who helped me to shape the original concept for the book.

To the team at Robinson; my copy-editor Sandra Ferguson, managing editor Amanda Keats, and my commissioning editor Duncan Proudfoot, whose trust, good faith, and intellectual enthusiasm for the project enabled me to deliver a work true to my own imagination and values.

To Richard, whose simultaneous faith and dismissal, bad humour and tough love kept me at it through the mire.

And to all those whose who have taken me on dates through the years, from the deranged to the sublime. You have caused me to question whether each generation shared the same dating wows and woes, and thus inspired the book. Thank you.

Index

Index

Index

Index

'Psychological Society' 63–4
purity movement 218

Quant, Mary 155
Queen, The (newspaper) 51
Queer As Folk (TV show) 209

racial segregation 144–5
Rad, Sean 225–6
Raeder, Phyllis 168
ragtime 55
Rahn, Stephanie 165
Raine, Eliza 42
Rantzen, Esther 218–19
rape 36, 124–5
Raschen, Sam 97
rationing 115
Reader's Digest 141–2
'Red Barn murder' 5
Renold, Dr Emma 219
reputation 56, 58, 99–100
Reynolds, Debbie 148
Richards, Keith 160
Riddell, Fern 29
Riding, Laura 63
Rimmel 22
rock and roll 129–31
Rockers 154–5
Rodger, Eliot 224
Roiphe, Katie 225
Rolling Stones 160, 171, 175
Rooke, Amelia 26
Roosevelt, Franklin D. 123
Rules, The (1995) 206
Russell, Bertrand 108
Russell, Christabel 81–2
Russell, John Hugo 81–2
Russell, Willy 195
Ryan, Meg 191

Sackville-West, Vita 89–90
St John, Florence 54
Sanger, Margaret 86
Schofield, Michael 151, 180
'season' 5, 30, 55, 95–6
Second Life 221, 229
'self-made girls' 47
Sellers, Edith 68
Sex and the City 205
sex education 61–2, 87, 117, 138–9, 151, 165, 168, 218
Sex for the Engaged (1952) 139–41
sex manuals 86, 107–8, 177
Sex in Our Time (TV series) 174

sex parties 231
Sex and the Single Girl (2003) 157
sex tourism 42, 212
Sexual Freedom League 163
Sexual Question, The (1908) 56
Sexual Revolution 147, 159
sexually transmitted infections (STIs) (venereal diseases) 61–2, 64, 72–3, 75, 99, 116, 122, 138, 172, 181, 225, 230–1
Shirley Valentine 195, 212
Silverstone, K. A. 172
Simpson, Wallis 97–8
Sinatra, Frank 129
singletons 74–5, 95, 100–1, 203–4, 216
Smell Dating 233
Smith, Geoffrey 91
Smyth, William Ernest 91
Snowdon, Lord 134
social mobility 18–19, 132
social purity 73–4
Spare Rib magazine 160–1, 167
Spears, Britney 218
SpeedDating 211
Stack, Mary Bagot 101
Star (fanzine) 171–2
Stead, W. T. 45
Steele, Danielle 194–5
Steinem, Gloria 159
stereoscopes 39
stockings 115–16, 120, 121, 122
Stopes, Marie 35, 86–7, 105
Strachey, Lytton 64
Strauss, Neil 223, 224
Student Christian Movement 108
Suffragettes 64–5, 75, 167
Sun (newspaper) 165, 197
Sunday Express (newspaper) 84–5, 109
Sunday Times (newspaper) 154, 178
swinging 162–3, 173
syphilis 44, 62, 64

Taber, Jean 111
Tangye, Lady Marguerite 75
Tarr, Jeffrey 163
Tatchell, Peter 170, 220
Tatham, Alex 189–90
Tatham, Sue 189–90
Taylor, Amy 221
Taylor, Elizabeth 148
Taylor, Samuel 43
tea dances 84
tea shops 74
'tea time' 56